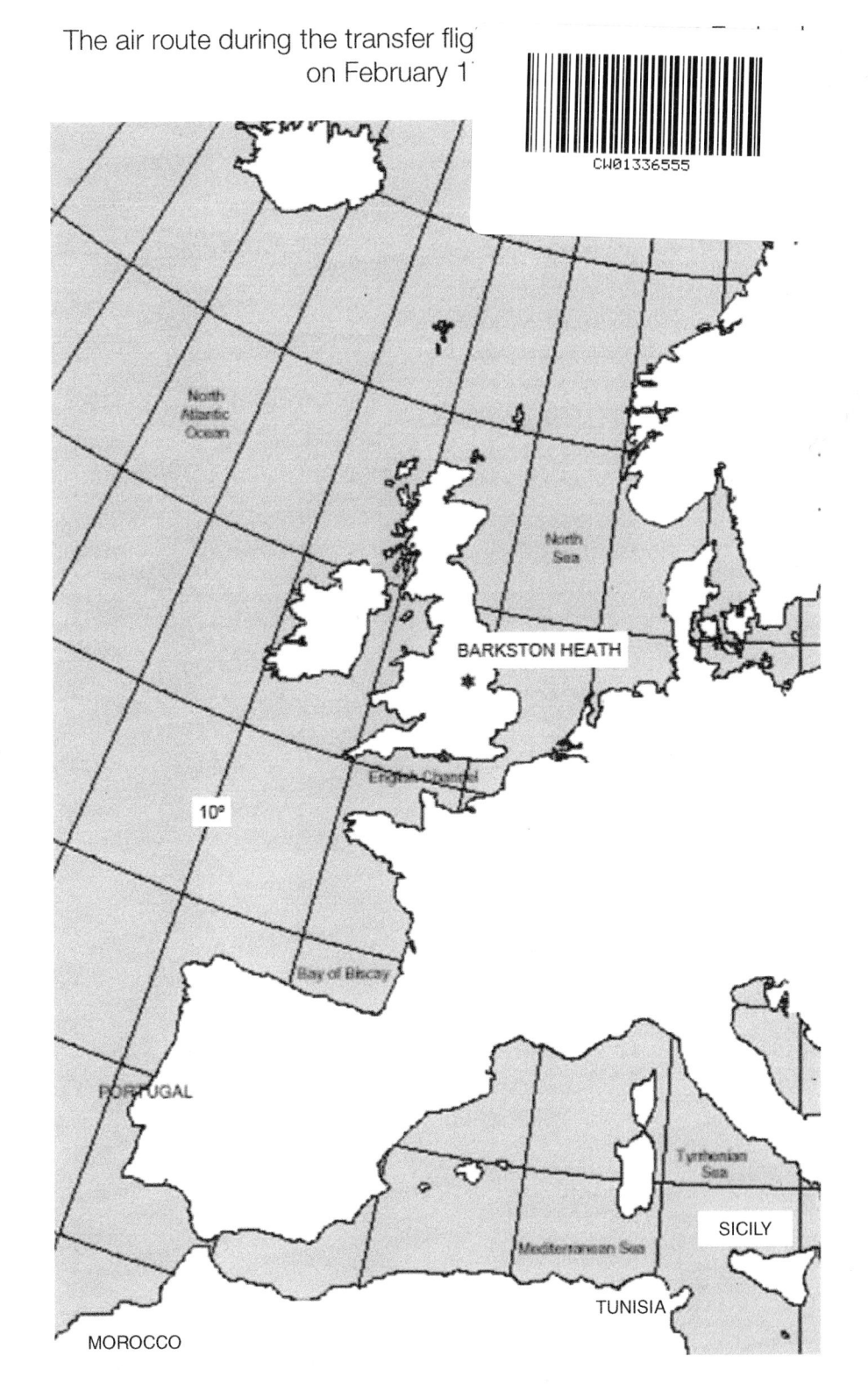

The air route during the transfer flight
on February 1

Christer Bergström

DAISY

The History of a C-47/DC-3 in World War II and the Men who Flew it

Dedicated to Oland Jones and Herbert Hassell
– they jumped into eternity

Copyright © 2018 and 2019 Christer Bergström
All rights reserved. No part of this book may be reproduced or transmitted in any form or by any means, electronic or mechanical, including photocopying, recording, or by any information storage and retrieval system, without permission in writing from the author. Requests for permission to make copies of any part of the work should be mailed to forlag@vaktelforlag.se

VAKTEL FÖRLAG

Some previous books by Christer Bergström
Luftwaffe Fighter Aircraft in Profile, 1997
Deutsche Jagdflugzeuge, 1999
Black Cross/Red Star: The Air War over the Eastern Front, vol. 1, 2000
Black Cross/Red Star: The Air War over the Eastern Front, vol. 2, 2001
More Luftwaffe Fighter Aircraft in Profile, 2002
Graf & Grislawski: A Pair of Aces, 2003
Jagdwaffe: Barbarossa—The Invasion of Russia, 2003
Jagdwaffe: The War in Russia January–October 1942, 2003
Jagdwaffe: The War in Russia November 1942–December 1943, 2004
Jagdwaffe: War in the East 1944–1945, 2005
Black Cross/Red Star: The Air War over the Eastern Front, vol. 3, 2006
Barbarossa: The Air Battle, 2007
Stalingrad: The Air Battle, 2007
Kursk: The Air Battle, 2008
Hans-Ekkehard Bob, 2008
Max-Hellmuth Ostermann, 2008
Bagration to Berlin, 2008
The Ardennes 1944–1945: Hitler's Winter Offensive, 2014
The Battle of Britain—An Epic Battle Revisited, 2015
Arnhem 1944—An Epic Battle Revisited. Vol. 1: Tanks and Paratroopers, 2019
Black Cross/Red Star: The Air War over the Eastern Front, vol. 4, 2019

Photographs, front cover: Björn Hellenius, Norbert Moh, Blomdal Family.
The airplane profile on the back cover depicts Daisy at the end of April 1944 and was made by Jim Laurier.

© 2018 and 2019 Christer Bergström
This edition of DAISY—The History of a C-47/DC-3 in World War II and the Men who Flew it first published 2019.
First published in Swedish by Vaktel Förlag 2018.
Original Swedish edition: Flygplanet Daisy i andra världskriget: en veteran och männen som flög henne i strid, berättat för första gången.
Cover design: Dennis Rudd dennis@kavitagraphics.co.uk
Graphic design: Henny Östlund henny.ostlund@gmail.com
Aircraft profile: Jim Laurier
Print: Printon Printing House, Estland
ISBN 978-91-88441-51-5

Vaktel förlag
Box 3027
630 03 Eskilstuna
Sweden
www.vaktelforlag.se
forlag@vaktelforlag.se

Table of Contents

Preface by Cheryl Grau and Shelley O'Connell, daughters of Norbert D. Moh, Daisy's Pilot During the War	6
Introduction by Tom D. Martin	8
Acknowledgements	9
D-Day	10
The Aviator—Norbert Moh	21
The Aircraft—Daisy	37
Daisy and Moh Fly to England	43
The Air Base—Barkston Heath	51
Arnhem	70
Daisy Flies On	100
Appendix 1: Video Section	103
Appendix 2: Daisy's Flights 1943-1945	106
Appendix 3: Specifications for Douglas C-47A Skytrain	115
Sources	116
Notes	117

Maps

The flight route on D-Day, 6 June 1944	Inside cover
The flight route during the transfer from Morocco to England on 17 February 1944	1
The flight route during Operation Market Garden, 17 September 1944	126-127

Preface

by Cheryl Grau and Shelley O'Connell, Daughters of Norbert D. Moh, Who Flew Daisy During the War

We are impressed and feel greatly honored for our father that Christer Bergström wrote such a detailed and wonderful book. The style of narrative makes you feel that you are really there with him for the trials and triumphs they all shared. The book is truly a treasure for all the World War II fans.

Our father Norbert Moh was certainly not one to talk about the war all the time. I've found that very few men did, but little things did come up ever so often. He told us about a bell necklace he bought in Capri during the war that he gave me, Cheryl, when I was very little. When I started studying French, he told me about the word "allez" which they used often for the little Arab boys who were always vying for attention. It seemed like during the leave time he was granted, he found his love for travel, even in those hard times. Most of all we were impressed about the lifelong friends he made, whom we would sometimes visit on our vacations, like Bill Metcalf and Homer Pottenger.

Although Dad was a German-speaking 3rd generation German immigrant, he was very proud to be an American, and he knew the government of Germany was corrupt and threatened freedom. He had no conflict in entering the war against Nazi Germany.

He remained interested and active in the governing of freedom even after the war. He was a captain in the Iowa Caucuses which was nationally watched during presidential election years as an indicator of how the country would vote, and he remained in the National Guard for many years.

Dad also kept up his pilot's license, and continued to be an instructor—a role which he loved. He eventually joined a Cessna coop which gave him the opportunity to fly more just for pleasure.

He never lost his love for travel and adventure. After he left the Air Traffic Control job, as a travel agent he was able to fly all over the world. From the candid pictures he took during the war, one could see his true interest humanity and the beauty of God's earth. His travels during that time took him full circle—back to Barkston Heath.

Our deepest thanks to our Dad, Norbert, as well as all the heroic men and women of WWII who put God and country ahead of themselves. They were ordinary people living in extraordinary times called to perform extraordinary deeds. Bound by the spirit of American camaraderie and a common goal, they united to victory. Because of their sacrifice we were able to grow up in a more safe and secure world. Thanks also to Daisy and the fleet of C-47's that supported the Allied victory.

Cheryl Grau and Shelley O'Connell
Daughters of Norbert D. Moh, Pilot of Daisy during the war,
Summerville, South Carolina, November 7, 2018

Introduction

by Tom D. Martin

My dad was a C-47 pilot in the 14th Troop Carrier Squadron of the US Air Force for the time that it was overseas during World War II. During the several years that I have researched his military service I have been fortunate to make contact with the families of many of his squadron mates. Early this year (2018) I learned that Daisy—a 14th Squadron C-47—survives in Sweden and that the author was planning a book on her history. I am happy that I was able to give the author some research help, and also put him into contact with the children of three of the men in Daisy's aircrew. Because of them, The Aircraft Daisy in World War II has a human element that makes it a most enjoyable book.

T.D. Martin,
El Lago, Texas, November 2, 2018

Acknowledgements

This book would never have been realized in its current shape had it not been for the fantastic help that several people have assisted me with during the course of my work. I would especially like to thank two people who have left a deep impression on the contents of the book: Tom Martin, son of a unit comrade of Norbert Moh, has opened many doors to incredibly valuable treasures about Daisy during World War II; Cheryl (Moh) Grau, daughter of Daisy's pilot Norbert Moh, has assisted me with fantastic material for the book, not least a large number of never previously published images from Norbert Moh's photo album, and Norbert Moh's written reminiscences.

Other people who have left important contributions to this book, and to whom I am therefore greatly indebted, are:

Lori Berdak Miller, researcher at NARA
Paul Blomdal, son of Arvid J. Blomdal
John Burgess, Grantham Journal Niclas Bååth, pilot of Daisy
Keane A. Carpenter, Capt, USAF
Shelley O'Connell, daughter of Daisy's pilot Norbert Moh
Stanley D. Gohl, DAFC 437th Airlift Wing Historian Brett Grau, son-in-law of Daisy's pilot Norbert Moh
Kevin King, son of a unit comrade of Daisy's pilot Norbert Moh, Marvin Krause
Diane Kunz, relative of Oland Jones Patricia Overman
Catherine Roberts, daughter of Charles N. Fay

Last but not least, I would like to extend my great thanks to my family, whose support and understanding I am privileged to always have: Maria, Caroline, Bambi, Albin, Benjamin, Bianca and my mother Britta.

Christer Bergström
Eskilstuna, Sweden, November 5, 2018

D-Day

Just after midnight on June 6, 1944, the people all over the vast area between Lincoln and Leicester were awoken by a great roar from sixteen hundred and forty-four powerful aircraft engines. Eight hundred and twenty-two American transport aircraft, most of them Douglas C-47 Skytrains, took off from nine different airfields, growling in a long, extended formation south-eastward. They carried more than 13,000 men from the 82nd and 101st U.S. Airborne Divisions. These would, together with British airborne forces, initiate the great invasion of Normandy, Operation "Neptune." This was D-Day.

One of the participating transport aircraft was the 61st Troop Carrier Group, which carried Lieutenant Colonel Charles Timmes's 2nd Battalion of the 507th Parachute Infantry Regiment from General Mark Gavin's 82nd Airborne Division.[1] Colonel Willis W. Mitchell, the Group's C.O., remembered, "My formation is assembled now and on-course flying at 1,500 feet underneath threatening clouds with a. spot of rain now and then. I cannot help but think – if only Hitler knew what was in store for him as this spearhead of the knock-out blow is about to fall on him, that he would probably give up. But I guess not since his fanatical mind could react as a tiger does when he's cornered. Anyway, here we go with one of the first punches. 1,250 paratroopers – the toughest, and without a doubt, the best trained infantry in the world today – aboard 72 C-47's [sic]. These boys are armed to the teeth and fighting mad. Their morale is at its peak. If we can only get them to the spot inside the dark, locked-up European continent, I'm sure they will do the rest."[2]

Eighteen of 61st Troop Carrier Group's aircraft were included in one of its subordinate squadrons, 14th Troop Carrier Squadron, under Major Lewis S. Frederick. Eighteen men from Lieutenant Colonel Timmes's battalion sat packed together on each side of the aircraft's aisle behind the cockpit in Aircraft 43-30732. A few hours earlier, this had had the number "24" written onto it in white chalk just next to the cargo hatch, so that the men would know which aircraft that was "theirs." Three of the eighteen men were sergeants, one was a corporal, and the rest were privates:

> Staff Sergeant Odis Plemmons
> Technical Sergeant Robert Carlquist
> Technical Sergeant Lambert Johnson
> Corporal Lawrence Cessna
> Private First Class Preston Hughes
> Private First Class Oland Jones
> Private First Class James Larkin
> Private First Class Charles Ward
> Private Joseph Dahlia
> Private Dominick De Midio
> Private James Dupuy
> Private Herbert Hassell
> Private Joseph Leporati
> Private Sylvester Pauxtis
> Private Joseph Pellegino
> Private Milford Pullen
> Private George S. Smedberg
> Private Victor Tomko

Most of them belonged to E Company, but some of them were from G Company of the battalion's staff group. Apart from these paratroopers, each aircraft carried six so-called parapacks underneath them, parachute canisters with equipment for the soldiers.

The pilot of 43-30732 was the 24-year-old 1st Lieutenant Norbert Moh from Wisconsin. To his right was the co-pilot, 2nd Lieutenant Ernest M. Martzen. In the space behind them was the radio operator Sergeant Arvid John Blomdal and the flight engineer Staff Sergeant William Gray.[3] The flight went at course 232 degrees, past the blacked-out cities of Leicester and Coventry to the right. One of the

American paratroopers, 1st Lieutenant Malcolm Brannen, remembers, "It was just getting dark and all that we could see out of the small windows were a few fields and the guide lights on the other planes. We could make out the hedge rows, water and roads when we flew over them.

"After we had started flying, the men began to smoke and a few talked. I spoke a few words to SGT Peak and to CPL King S. Burke, one of the Battalion Intelligence Section NCOs, who was #15 in our stick. Then I tried t settle in a sleep. It was a fitful sleep and hard to continue what with the little bucket seat and the great big load we had to place there. The door through which we were going to leave the plane was wide open, making a bit cool inside."[4] The aircraft passed the "Atlanta" radio beacon, twenty miles east of Birmingham, and at the "Cleveland" beacon between Ledbury and Cheltenham, the formation turned left to course 184 degrees"I just snuggled down

2nd Lieutenant Homer K. Pottenger's Douglas C-47 at the Barkston Heath airbase. (Photo: Norbert Moh. Via Cheryl Moh Grau.)

in the seat as far as I could," Brannen recounts. "It really didn't help much. Soon we were over the marsh lands."

After 26 minutes, the aircraft reached the "Elko" beacon, and there, they turned yet again towards southwest, 213 degrees, sweeping after 13 minutes at an altitude of 150 meters past the Portland Bill lighthouse on the grassy isthmus stretching out from Weymouth, and flying out over the English Channel. The weather over the Channel was clear, and all formations were kept together well. Brannen remembers, "The channel was beautiful with the moon reflecting on it and making it look all silvery and made me think of the moon and the reflection on the Atlantic seashore at home. But it also looked cold and uninviting."

Four minutes after flying out over the sea, the pilots turned off their position lights, which had been switched on until then to facilitate formation flight.[5] "By this time", Brannen recounted, "all cigarettes were out and no lights were showing inside the plane. We were getting into bombing range and one wee light showing might give the whole formation away and possibly disrupt the entire operation." In Moh's aircraft, the flight engineer, Gray, walked around among the paratroopers, checking that no cigarettes or other luminous spots were lit. Twenty minutes later, the aircraft reached "Hoboken", a so-called "Eureka" transmitter on a ship 55 miles out in the Channel, signaling that the aircraft had reached the point where they were to turn left to course 125 degrees. There, Moh and the other pilots also switched off their warning lights underneath. Now, only the formation lights were lit. These consisted of three small lights on top of each wing. These were screened off, so that they could only be seen if you were at the correct position in the formation. These, too, were now dimmed to their weakest luminosity.

Moh's aircraft was positioned as number three in a V formation with Captain John W. Hagey's 42-24267 at the front and 2nd Lieutenant Homer K. Pottenger's 42-32834, nicknamed "Sprag Wagon", to the right. They were positioned diagonally to the right behind Squadron Commander Frederick's leading three-plane

V formation.[6] Being the pilot, Moh could not take his eyes off the nearest aircraft in the formation, even for a brief moment—he could not even take a quick glance at the instrument panel to see which speed, altitude, course, engine power or anything else that his aircraft had. All such things had to be taken care of for him by Martzen, the co-pilot.[7] 1st Lieutenant Clyde E. Roach, another pilot in Moh's unit, recounted, "Vertigo (dizziness combined with lack of orientation with the environment) was quite common, except in the lead ship. We developed a method of combating vertigo by having the pilot who was not flying to continually talk, giving airspeed, altitude, turn, climb, etc. If you believe your companion, the signals to the brain would straighten out the same as if you glanced at the flight instruments. Part of our training for this mission was a night vision class. In a blacked out hangar, you literally could not see your hand in front of your face, white lines were painted on the floor and white bean bags were strewn around. We were asked to walk the lines and pick up the bags. The first night it was almost impossible, but after being taught how best to utilize the eyes, it was easy. Of course wearing red goggles for three hours before the exercise helped."[8]

Ten minutes after the turn at "Hoboken", the aircraft passed right between the two Channel Islands of Guernsey and Alderney, on their way straight towards the French coast on the Cotentin Peninsula. A few tracers from flak on the Channel Islands rose towards the aircraft, but it was all badly aimed. The aircraft now ascended, and presently, Moh asked Flight Engineer Gray to inform the paratroopers that it was 20 minutes to the target. Altitude was the ordered 460 meters as the aircraft crossed the French coast, 23 minutes after the turn over "Hoboken." There, they entered thick clouds covering the entire western part of the Cotentin Peninsula. This was where the problems began. Until then, the formations had been kept in the clear weather, but now, the aircraft were hit by both clouds and strong turbulence— and, in addition, by unexpectedly strong German flak. Brannen remembers, "Soon the coast of France came along – along with dull pounding of ack ack guns and flak guns. The plane began to pitch,

Colonel Willis W. Mitchell, commander of 61st Troop Carrier Group, and (right) the Assistant Group Commander, Lieutenant Commander Stanley C. Hoyt. The image is taken in front of one of the unit's C-47 Skytrains at Barkston Heath on 18 April 1944. (Photo: Norbert Moh. Via Cheryl Moh Grau.)

roll and bump as a toy boat on a turbulent stream, and we were being bumped about quite a bit. No one was saying much – just asking if each other was okay, or, 'Did you hear that one?' meaning flak or tracer bullets from the enemy guns below us.

"Meanwhile, there had been quite a bit of commotion at the rear of our plane. We, in the front, couldn't quite see or hear enough of it to understand... Later, I found out that when we had passed between Jersey and Guernsey Islands and received the 20-minutes-to-drop warning, PVT Calhoun said to our jump master, CPT Bell, 'My parachute has broken open.' In the brief space of less than 20 minutes, Calhoun was relieved of his equipment and parachute – the rear of which had broken open. Another parachute was substituted and all equipment replaced so that he was ready to go and did jump with the rest of us."

Then, the red light indicating that the target was four minutes away went on. "Our C-47 was now bounding around in the air (really bounding)," Brannen recounted. "[It was] going up and down and it seemed as if we were bucking ocean waves rather than air turbulence. Our jump master, CPT Bell let out a yell. 'Stand up and hook up' – and at once 18 arms struck at the anchor line cable with their static line snap fastener. It took some of us a bit longer to hook up than it did others because we were so crowded with 18 men in line, having such loads attached to us, and also because the plane was resembling a bucking bronco and that cable line just wouldn't stay in place! Finally, we were all hooked up. Then we were checked and all reported as all set – 'okay.'"

Moh held on as hard as he could to the yoke while struggling with the turbulence in the fog, which was constantly lit by exploding anti-aircraft grenades. He was guided towards the drop zone by the aircraft's "Rebecca" radio, which received signals from the "Eureka" transmitters that were operated by Pathfinders—the paratroopers who had landed first of all to lead the rest or the aircraft to the right positions. But no markings of the drop zone—which should have been there both in the shape of purple smoke and a large "T" made up by white sheets—were anywhere to be seen. German soldiers had prevented the Pathfinders from completing this task. In the ensuing confusion, the formations were broken up as the pilots turned back to look for markings that were not there. Many crews went back as many as three times before eventually switching on the green light as a sign for the paratroopers to jump. 1st Lieutenant George R. Hull from the ground crew of the 61st TCG recounts, "The pilots told of seeing thousands of ships and planes; of seeing harmless haystacks spit fire as the C-47s approached; of seeing buildings explode and airplanes crash; of seeing tanks and men battling below."[9] Different aircraft gave the order to jump at different times and in different places. Brannen recalled, "I was holding onto the cable line for dear life and my hands, my right one on the cable line and my left one on the snap fastener, were nearly being wrenched free of their holdings.

My right arm was nearly ripped from its socket. It seemed we couldn't hold on much longer, nor could we stand upright much longer.

"Let's go! The green light came on – just a thin slit of the bulb was showing so as not to make too much light in the airplane."[10] Another soldier of 507th Parachute Infantry Regiment, Howard Huebner, remembers, "We knew the area where we were supposed to land, because we had studied it on sand tables, and then had to draw it on paper by memory, but that all faded as our regiment was the last to jump, and things had changed on the ground. Most of us missed our drop zone by miles. As we were over our drop zone there was a downed burning plane. Later I found out it was one of ours. The flack [sic] was hitting our plane and everything from the ground coming our way looked like the Fourth of July." One of the men who jumped from Norbert Moh's aircraft, Private Joseph Dahlia from E Company, recounts, "We jumped, we were scattered all over the countryside. Our full platoon did not assemble. My jump was good. I landed in a cow pasture in a pile of manure. As I was coming down, I could see some movement on the ground. For one moment I thought they were all Germans, but to my surprise, no Germans. Just cows."[11]

It was about half past two in the morning of 6 June 1944. However, everyone from the 507th Parachute Infantry Regiment did not make it that well. During the seconds when the paratroopers were falling to the ground, and the men were looking down, they first thought they were seeing ordinary fields and arable lands below them, but when they got closer, many of them discovered that it was water! The Germans had flooded the river Merderet, and several paratroopers hit the water. Some of them ended up in water that was several meters deep, drowning helplessly, weighed down as they were by their heavy kits. Others ended up in water that was only knee-deep, and were able to wade to higher ground.

The aircraft of 61st Group dropped their paratroopers in completely chaotic conditions between 0226 and 0245 hrs, or perhaps even later.[12]

Joseph Dahlia from E Company continues his story, "We were scattered all over the countryside. Our full platoon did not assemble. The first buddy I came across was Sergeant Johnson." In the dark, Dahlia and Lambert Johnson joined six other men who had jumped from Norbert Moh's airplane: Robert Carlquist, James Dupuy, Sylvester Pauxtis, Oland Jones, Herbert Hassell and Dominick De Midio. They were all cold and disoriented. Dahlia was wounded by a bullet that ricocheted off his rifle and hit his left hand. He recounts, "Private 1st Class Demidion from New Jersey administered first aid as the blood was all over. I think it severed an artery.

My weapon was out of commission. I was no help to them. So they left me. All I had was a knife and four grenades. After they were gone I managed to get to a French farmhouse where the people took care of me. But it wasn't long when two Germans came to the farmhouse looking for food. They found me and took me prisoner. They transported me by horse and buggy to a town about 11km from the farmhouse and then to a German aid station that was set up in a Catholic monastery where I was operated on by a German doctor who amputated my left index finger and sewed my thumb back on and removed the metacarpal bone. The French doctor spoke English. He said, 'Are you an American?' I turned my right shoulder and showed him the American flag that was sewn on my sleeve. The doctor told me he received part of his medical training at the University of Chicago and he was a guest of the late Cardinal Mundelion. After the operation I found myself in a room with six other wounded Americans."[13]

While this was going on, Moh and the other pilots were steering their aircraft away from the drop zone, veering at increased throttle to the left while the flak continued firing at them. They arced the northern coast of the Cotentin Peninsula, continued while climbing to an altitude of about 1,000 meters, and took the same rout back as they had used for their approach after about half an hour.

1st Lieutenant Hull from the 61st TCG headquarters recounts from the Barkston Heath airfield, "At 0415, the transports started to return. They 'buzzed' the field with a mighty roar, and settled down one after the other. Some didn't return. Many of those that did return had their metal hides shot up with bullets."[14] The aviators were tired but happy—happy to have survived this important mission, happy to have survived. One of Norbert Moh's squadron comrades, the pilot and 1st Lieutenant James Shemas, recounts, "Major Lewis S. Frederick's face peered in from the entrance, smiling and confident. He and his crew were the first to come into the interrogation room. 'Well,' said Major Frederick as he sat down at Captain Arnold H. Newman's interrogation table, 'Europe's all invaded to hell.' And so Major Frederick and his crew told their story of their flight; more pilots and their crews started drifting in and the atmosphere hummed with the noise of busy men, became heavy with success, proud of a job well done… When the interrogations were finished, the crews got their breakfasts, and tried to get what sleep they could."[15]

Two of the eighteen men jumping from Norbert Moh's aircraft were killed during the Battle of Normandy: Oland Jones and Herbert Hassell. The 21-year-old Oland Jones was found dead on June 7 or 8, but the person who first buried him misread his dog tag. It was only when his remains were later disinterred for a more proper funeral that his identity could be established. Today, he is buried at the City Cemetery at Guntersville, Marshall County, Alabama, USA. His sister Ruby, six years his junior, passed away as late as in 2017. Herbert Hassell, who was killed on June 6, is buried today at the American military cemetery in Colleville-sur-Mer in Normandy, Plot E, 24:33. Charles Ward was killed just before the end of the war, on April 15, 1945, but fifteen out of the eighteen survived the war. The last one of them, George S. Smedberg, passed away in June 2012.

Oland Jones (left) with his sister Christine and brother Warren. (Via Diane Kunz.)

A letter written by Oland Jones to his sister Louise in May, 1944, one month before his death. (Via Diane Kunz.)

The Aviator — Norbert Moh

Norbert Delmar Moh was born on his parents' farm, six miles east of Granton, Wisconsin, on November 30, 1919. He was a third-generation immigrant; both of his parents were of German descent, to be precise, from Bavaria. His paternal grandfather had been fighting for the Union in the American Civil War and had also been involved in the Indian wars. Norbert's parents spoke German, and they also

Norbert Moh. (Norbert Moh's photo album. Via Cheryl Moh Grau.)

let Norbert be taught German in school. In 1934, he graduated from junior high school with the highest grades of all the students. After that, he attended high school in Granton. Twenty-two years old, he enlisted in March 1942, for service in the U.S. Army Air Corps. At enlistment, he was 5' 6" and weighed 170 lbs. His eye color was registered as gray and his hair color was brown.

When he enlisted, Moh had never sat in an aircraft before. Following his basic military training at Santa Ana, California, he was sent to aviation school in Visalia, California, where he learned to fly in Ryan PT-22s and Vultee BT-13 Valiant aircraft. One air exercise almost cost him his life; it was when he went down in a tailspin with a Vultee. However, after having lost about 5,000 feet of altitude, he managed to get the machine up again. Having completed basic aviation training, he was transferred to Stockton, where he learned advanced flight in an AT-6 Texan. It was a demanding training, which only 20 % of the candidates made it through, but on October 30, 1942, Moh graduated as a full-fledged pilot and 2nd Lieutenant.

Moh was selected to become a transport aircraft pilot and was given special DC-3 training in Austin, Texas, and Whiteman Sedalia, Missouri. Even though it was military training, he and the other rookie pilots had to practice in civilian DC-3s with their passenger seats still in place, and the flight instructors were also former commercial pilots.

Having completed this, he was sent on to Dalhart, Texas, where he was trained in towing gliders. Moh remembered that the cockpit heater was constantly broke, so that he and the others had to fly dressed in thick sheepskin furs. During one of his night flights, the glider that he was towing became disconnected, and crashed into a slaughterhouse—the only building around for fifty miles! At the venerable Fort Bragg, he was finally trained in flying parachuting missions. During this time, he married his betrothed May Hirschberg in Dalhart, Texas.

On May 3, 1943, Moh, now promoted to 1st Lieutenant, reported to a transport aviation division of the U.S. Army Air Force, the

Norbert and May Moh's wedding photo in Dalhart, Texas, on January 21, 1943. (Via Cheryl Moh Grau.)

Norbert Moh during his training in Visalia. (Norbert Moh's photo album. Via Cheryl Moh Grau.)

14th Troop Carrier Squadron, at Morrison Field close to Palm Beach, Florida. Together with the 15th, 53rd, and 59th Squadrons, the 14th Troop Carrier Squadron were part of the 61st Troop Carrier Group under Colonel Willis W. Mitchell. Together with the 314th Troop Carrier Group, this group formed the 52nd Troop Carrier Wing commanded by the forty-nine-year-old Colonel Harold L. Clark.

The 14th Troop Carrier Squadron was called "The Pelicans" and had a light blue pelican with a paratrooper jumping from its beak as a unit symbol. Squadron commander was Major Lewis S. Frederick. The entire group was equipped with Douglas C-47 Skytrain transport aircraft—the military, but yet unarmed, version of the commercial DC-3 aircraft. Each squadron had twelve such aircraft as a standard, but the 14th Squadron had thirteen when Moh arrived.

By then, the German and the Italian last stronghold in Northern Africa—a small bridgehead in northern Tunisia—was facing its imminent fall. As early as at the Casablanca conference in January, 1943, the leaders of the Western Allies had decided that the next step after conquering Northern Africa would be landing on Sicily. The plan that was drawn up for this, Operation "Husky," was based on a seaborne landing combined with an effort by airborne soldiers who were to be landed by gliders and parachutes.

Ahead of this operation, the 52nd Troop Carrier Wing was ordered to regroup right across the Atlantic and into Northern Africa.

Moving across the Atlantic was no simple task, but a careful plan was drawn up. All aircraft were equipped with four extra fuel tanks in the fuselage, so-called "Bolero Tanks." Together with the ordinary fuel tanks, these gave the C-47s a flying time of 12 hours non-stop at cruising speed. The "Southern Route," via the Caribbean, South America, and West Africa, was chosen. This provided the shortest distance across the Atlantic.[16]

On May 3, 1943, the same day as Moh's arrival, all thirteen aircraft in the 14th Squadron took off for the first leg of the long flight, which took them to San Juan, the capital of Puerto Rico, the American possession in the Caribbean. The following day, Moh and the other aviators took off from there, continuing towards the South American mainland. Moh was at the controls of the aircraft # 41-18384. The co-pilot of this airplane was William Jay Metcalf, the reserve pilot was Charles Schafer, the crew chief was Chester Dwight Urban, and the radio operator was William Curtis Twitty. A person named Nolan Thomas Kirby was also on the plane as a passenger.[17]

Sergeant 1st Class Virgil L. Cox, another of the unit's transport pilots, recounted, "We left Puerto Rico for Atkinson Field in British Guiana. Arrived there at 1:30 p.m. I picked up some of their currency as a souvenir. It was my first sight of jungle land and it sure looked 'spooky.'"[18] On May 5, the journey continued, this time towards Brazil. Cox continues his account, "Left British Guiana on way south. Flew over more water, jungle, and swamp land. We landed in Belem [sic], Brazil at 11:45 a.m. Weather was hot and sticky. We crossed the Amazon river on the way down. It is easy to understand why it is the world's largest river. I have never seen anything to compare with it. Spent my first night under a mosquito bar. I don't like the smell of Brazil but I guess that is just the beginning."

From Belém, Cox, Moh, and the other pilots continued to Natal on the northeastern tip of Brazil. There, they had a few days' rest to prepare everything ahead of the flight across the Atlantic. Cox recounts, "Went swimming at the beach this evening—sure was swell. The natives swarmed us with food to sell such as bananas and watermelons. I bought two bunches of bananas for 50 cents which was cheap to me but high to them. These natives are nobody's fool. Bought two knives as souvenirs from a native. The big one sure is handy." The next day, some of the Americans went to town. They found it interesting, even if there was not much to do there.

On May 8, Moh made the risky flight across the Atlantic Ocean. After ten hours' flight—of which Moh took half and the co-pilot half—they landed as planned on Ascension Island in the middle of the Atlantic.[19] The following day, they continued their flight across the sea due north. More than seven hours later, they landed in Freetown, Sierra Leone. On May 19, they continued to Dakar, Senegal, which was controlled by France. They stayed there for two days.[20] Dakar was one of the most important offloading stations for the military traffic between the United States and North Africa/southern Europe during World War II. Lieutenant William I. Marlatt recounted, "We laid over a day at Dakar for a 25-hour engine inspection. Some of us took the bus into the city of Dakar and wandered around. The bus was an old Chevrolet at least 20 years old with a wooden body somewhat like a school bus. There was no glass in the windows and several of the floorboards were broken out, so that one could look out and see the ground. Dakar was a fairly nice-looking place. The streets were paved and there were sidewalks. There were shrubs and flowers, so they must have irrigated them. On the way back to the airfield the bus met a group of black women and kids, who had apparently been fishing. The women were carrying fish balanced on their heads. The fish looked something like big bass or carp, weighing perhaps 20 pounds. They did their best to sell them to us as the bus crept past them."[21]

In the morning of May 12, the entire unit took off for the goal for the next stage, Marrakesh, Morocco. They flew via Tindouf, Algeria, in order to avoid neutral Spain's airspace over Spanish Morocco

Norbert Moh ahead of a flight with a Ryan PT-22 Recruit training aircraft at the Visalia airfield in California. (Norbert Moh's photo album. Via Cheryl Moh Grau.)

(today's West Sahara). The sky was clear, but large dust clouds just above the ground obscured downwards visibility during most of the flight. Eventually, however, the dust clouds disappeared, and the vast, empty desert spread out beneath the airmen. After a few hours, they flew past the Atlas Mountains, which they found almost absurdly green after all the sand dunes, and some snow was visible on the highest peaks. Here, the air was quite cold. After almost nine hours' flight—of which the last two were in the dark—the unit landed at the airport in Marrakesh (known today as Marrakesh Minara).[22] Captain Augustine T. S. Stoney wrote, "That night practically everyone went into the city to see and smell, (but do very little tasting of), the unfamiliar foreigners. Some on foot, some in ancient Victoria or Hoover buggies."[23]

In the morning of May 13, 1943, the whole unit took off again, landing after a 90-minute flight at its new permanent base, Lourmel in northern Morocco. At this site, about 30 miles from Oran, the Americans had set up an air base in a few old wheat fields immediately after the landings in Morocco and Algeria in November 1942. This consisted of a concrete runway, concrete aprons, and a hangar. As for staff accommodation, there was nothing else than tents, and water had to be fetched from the nearby village of Lourmel.

The only relief from boredom for the airmen was going the ten miles to a fantastic sandy beach that was sandwiched in between the cliffs on the Mediterranean coast. They went there on trucks each night to wash off the desert dust.

At the very same moment that the 52nd Troop Carrier Wing landed in Lourmel, the last German-Italian resistance in Tunisia was broken. 230,000 men were taken captive in the largest surrender involving German units during Second World War II.

The 52nd Troop Carrier Wing now had 159 Douglas C-47 Skytrains ready to be deployed into the invasion of Sicily. On May 20, the troop transport ship *USS West Point* arrived at the port of Casablanca with the ground crew, 4,800 men, and all equipment for the group. The ship had sailed all across the Atlantic unescorted, zigzagging to avoid any U-boat attacks.[24] During the following days, Moh and the other pilots shuttled back and forth to Casablanca with staff and equipment.[25] When this was completed, they continued flying equipment and staff from different ports to other airports. Then, intense training followed. The airmen practiced dropping paratroopers and gliders, and formation flight at night.

On June 15, a reconnaissance force of two officers and 30 troops flew from the 14th Squadron to what would become the unit's new advance airbase, eight miles northwest of Kairouan in Tunisia. There, an airfield had been constructed only recently. The first unit to operate from there was the 14th Squadron. The men of the unit found the airbase to be nothing else than a great, sage-covered plain. Quarters consisted of tents here as well, large pyramid tents that had been erected in pairs, with 100 yards between each pair. For security reasons, the aircraft were parked 300 yards apart. Pits in the ground covered by oil barrels that had been split in two down the middle were the only protection against airstrikes. In addition, there were some British anti-aircraft guns.[26] All units included in the 52nd Wing were dispersed across similar fields at least four miles apart, so that the various units could land in the dark simultaneously.

Lieutenant William I. Marlatt recounted, "This was desert, but not sand. Kairouan was a holy city of Islam and we were instructed not to go there. At our landing strip there were no buildings within sight. It was hot and dry. The weeds were all dead. The enemy had retreated across this area on their way out of Africa in early May, six or seven weeks before we got there. There was just one road in this area, it was just a narrow asphalt strip running parallel to the

Street view from Lourmel, Morocco.

The unit badge of the 14th Troop Carrier Squadron. The edge was yellow, the fields navy blue, the beak orange, the parachutes white, and the men naked and beige. The bird's body and wings were light blue, while its rudder, bottom, and the front edge of its wings were white.

coast which was about ten miles further east. Several wrecked enemy planes were lying on the ground within a mile or two of our strip. They had either been shot down or they ran out of gas. Many of the tanks traveled here and there through the weedy countryside. A few miles west of our camp there was a German 88-mm gun, which had apparently been put out of commission by Allied aircraft fire. The German crew had apparently been killed, because there was blonde hair lying around on the ground and the smell of decaying flesh and some evidence that bodies might have been buried in shallow graves nearby... Along the narrow asphalt road I noticed a temporary grave where some enemy soldier had been buried and a stake driven in the ground to mark the grave."[27]

Training flights continued here, and each day, the C-47s' propellers whipped up great red clouds of dust, which covered everything and penetrated everything. Moh and the other airmen practiced towing gliders, dropping paratroopers, and transporting equipment, often at night.

On July 9, 1943, the time had finally come. Operation "Husky" was to commence that night. 227 C-47 Skytrains from the 52nd Troop Carrier Wing were standing by. They were to carry 3,405 paratroopers from the 82nd U.S. Airborne Division to Sicily.

The 14th Squadron had ten operational aircraft. The American paratroopers had their dinner at 1600 hours and then mounted trucks that took them to the various airfields around Kairouan. There, they were divided according to aircraft, 15 men in each. At

2000 hours, they were aboard the aircraft, and the pilots were ready for takeoff. At 2010 hours, the takeoff order came. With an almighty rumble, hundreds of engines were fired up, and while visibility was obscured by a quickly thickening dust cloud, the transport aircraft began taxiing out onto the runway, three by three.[28]

227 aircraft were rolling out for takeoff. 226 got up in the air and set off for enemy territory. Only one was unable to take off due to technical problems—and it was Norbert Moh's machine! He was forced to disembark and listen to the enormous mass of aircraft

Norbert Moh (front) and his comrades on the wall at the seafront in Sciacca. (Norbert Moh's photo album. Via Cheryl Moh Grau.)

taking off—he had to *listen* to them, but could not see them, as the dust cloud created by so many aircraft taking off was so great that paratroopers inside the aircraft could see it from four miles away.[29]

Apart from the mishap with Moh's aircraft, however, the operation during the night between July 9 and 10, 1943, was a complete success for the 14th Troop Carrier Squadron. In spite of strong side winds, all airborne aircraft reached the landing area, all paratroopers were dropped at exactly the right spots, and all aircraft returned safely to base.

In the evening of July 11, it was time again. The entire unit took off to fly in reinforcements to Sicily. This time, the 1st and 2nd Battalions of one of the 82nd Airborne Division's regiments, the 504th, were the ones that were going to jump at the Gela airbase. And this time, Moh was with them in one of a total of 144 Skytrains with 2,304 paratroopers.

Norbert Moh himself recounts, "We took off in the evening of what would become five hours' formation flight without any other light to guide is than the tongues of fire from the exhaust pipes and the full moon. We flew closely above the water so as to avoid being detected by radar. The Germans had surrounded the drop zones in Sicily with tanks and soldiers. Their heavy flak painted the sky red. Many paratroopers didn't reach the drop area but were scattered across the southern parts of the island. Our flight took us further inland than intended, in over an area that we didn't know. We barely escaped flying into a high mountain, and when sweeping by at low altitude, part of the cargo that we were carrying underneath the plane was torn off when colliding with the treetops. In spite of giving full throttle, we didn't reach more than 75 mph. Another unit didn't make it across the mountain but flew around it. My plane limped back to Africa with more than 500 bullet holes in it. None in the crew was wounded, but they broke down mentally and had to be sent home again."[30]

Returning to Kairouan, one of the aircraft from the 14th Squadron was missing, and in another lay the dead body of a paratrooper—

the result of a flak hit. In total, 23 of the participating transport aircraft were shot down during the night between July 11 and 12, 1943, and another 37 were badly damaged.[31] However, for the gallantry shown by the airmen, in spite of the heavy flak, the 14th Troop Carrier Squadron was awarded the kind of decoration for a unit that existed I the U.S. Army, the Distinguished Unit Citation. Even though the squadron continued flying missions over Sicily, Moh was grounded for five days—probably while his aircraft was being repaired. Meanwhile, the battle of the island went towards a victorious end for the Allies. Beginning on July 28, the 14th Squadron flew in supplies to the airfield at Palermo, Sicily, which the Americans had taken. Moh was spending the night between July 31 and August 1 in Palermo, just as the city harbor was subject to a major German bomb attack. Several ships were hit, gas and oil depots were set ablaze, and an ammunition train was blown up. "Spent the night in a foxhole," Moh wrote laconically.[32]

Norbert Moh in Sciacca, Sicily. (Norbert Moh's photo album. Via Cheryl Moh Grau.)

On August 10, Moh took the controls of one of the ten transport aircraft carrying the personnel of the 47th Bomb Group from Malta to its new airbase in Sicily.[33] With Sicily in Allied hands, the 14th Troop Carrier Squadron was moved forward to an airfield southwest of Djerba in south Tunisia, where intense practicing of glider landings on the beach followed.

On September 3, one of Moh's comrades, Charles Queale, was forced to ditch his C-47 in the Mediterranean. Queale and the five men that constituted the rest of the crew achieved the incredible feat of paddling their rubber boat to the Italian island of Pantelleria, which under Allied control.[34] Three days later, the squadron was shifted to an airfield at Licata, Sicily, this ahead of the Allied landing of the Italian mainland at the Gulf of Salerno. The landing took place on September 9, 1943. Fierce fighting raged for several days.

On September 12, Moh flew two missions to transport personnel and supplies from the 82nd Airborne Division from North Africa to Sicily.[35] The men of the 14th Squadron noticed that something big was underway when a fighter carrying a written order from General Mark Clark, Commander of the U.S. 5th Army, landed in Licata in the afternoon of September 13. Soon afterwards, the U.S. Paratrooper General Matthew B. Ridgway landed in Licata. The written order meant that the 52nd Troop Carrier Wing was to drop the 504th Parachute Infantry Regiment of the 82nd Airborne Division over the bridgehead at Salerno.

The same evening, the entire squadron flew with ten aircraft to Comiso, where they were briefed about the operation. The transport aircraft were to take off at 2040 hours and convene in the air over Cape Rasocolmo in northeastern Sicily. From there, they were to fly along the Italian west coast up towards the bridgehead at Salerno. The airmen were to be led to their target by pathfinders—paratroopers who had landed ahead of the main force—who for the first time were going to use the new "Eureka" equipment. These small portable transmitters sent out radio signals that were received by a complementary receiver, a so-called "Rebecca", which the aircraft had been equipped with. In addition, the landing zones were to be marked with burning gas cans that had been set up as a giant "T."[36]

Before the paratroopers boarded their aircraft, the American Regiment Commander told them, "The Krauts are kicking the shit out of our boys over at Salerno. We're going to jump into the beachhead tonight and rescue them. Put on your parachutes and get on the plane—we're taking off in a few minutes for the gates of hell."[37]

The mission was carried out with total success. The air crews intercepted the "Eureka" signals at between six and twelve miles from the target, and most of the paratroopers were dropped within 200 yards from the designated spot. The fact that the airborne units did not have any decisive influence on the battle was another issue; in any case, the Battle of Salerno ended with Allied victory as well.

At the end of September and beginning of October, 1943, Moh and other pilots from the 14th Troop Carrier Squadron flew fuel to Sardinia. One of these missions, September 29, was Moh's 100th sortie with a C-47 Skytrain.[38] On October 6, the unit was shifted to Sciacca, Sicily. Here, the ground was softer and less dusty. Again, the

Norbert Moh and orphans that the unit was helping at Sciacca, Sicily. (Norbert Moh's photo album. Via Cheryl Moh Grau.)

men were biletted in tents that had been erected in an olive grove some distance from the airfield.

Starting in October, a period of four and a half months of relative calm for the men ensued. No combat missions were flown, but on the other hand, some transport flights were made between North Africa and Sicily, or between Sicily and the airfield at Palermo. In order to kill the boredom, a bar for the airmen was opened in October, 1943, at the Sciacca airfield. There, the men could buy drinks for between 5 and 35 cents. The most popular one was gin and lemonade. Every now and then, the 61st Troop Carrier Group Dance Band played, led by the trumpeter and 2nd Lieutenant George Hull, an intelligence officer from the headquarters.[39]

On November 20, there was a large-scale glider exercise with all available aircraft and crews at Sciacca.

During the general uneventfulness, there were various rumors about what was awaiting the unit. One day, the word was that they were to be transferred to England for an invasion of France, another day, India was the destination, in order to fight the Japanese. Most of them agreed that things would be worse of they came to England— it would definitely not be as easy to come across fruit and vegetables there as in Sicily. One of the most fantastic rumors had it that President Roosevelt, Winston Churchill, and a representative of the German armed forces were holding secret negotiations in Cairo. One of the men swore that he had seen Roosevelt alight from an aircraft in Tunis.[40]

The aircraft — Daisy

While the war was raging in Europe, Asia, and the Pacific, the great and growing American manufacturing industry was working at full speed to provide the soldiers on the Allied side with the equipment that would give them the victory. The large government orders from the manufacturing industry made the U.S. gross domestic product skyrocket, from 800 billion dollars in 1938 to almost 1,500 billion in 1944. In comparison, Germany's GDP rose during the same period from the equivalent of 351 billion to 437 billion dollars (all figures in 1990 money).[41] The U.S. military production rose from 1,400 aircraft in 1941 to more than 54,000 aircraft in 1943. The latter figure was 50 % higher than Germany's and Japan's production put together.

It is often said that World War II brought the American women out into professional life. Indeed, the number of wage-earning women did increase from 14 million in 1940 to more than 19 million in 1945, but this number fell back to slightly more than 16 million after the war; it was only many decades later that the American woman would take the step out onto the labor market. However, in some areas, the number of female workers within the manufacturing industry soared. One of them was at the Douglas Aircraft Company in Long Beach, California: in January 1942, Douglas in Long Beach hired 500 women. One year later, their number had risen to more than 30,000! During the course of the war, the Long Beach would eventually employ more than 175,000 workers, 40 % of whom were women.[42]

With so many women employed, the Long Beach works became the epitome of "Rosie the Riveter," the female worker that Redd Evans and John Jacob Loeb wrote a very popular song about, performed by The Vagabonds. This inspired the iconic poster with a woman flexing her biceps saying "We Can Do It!"—the same poster that in later years has become a symbol of feminism.

The Long Beach works became the epitome of "Rosie the Riveter," the female worker who inspired the iconic wartime poster "We Can Do It!" which was intended to recruit women in the U.S. to the manufacturing industry during World War II.

The factory plant in Long Beach cost 12 million dollars to build. It was an ultramodern factory, fully adapted for war. As camouflage, the flat roofs were filled with fake residential houses made out of canvas on frames, "trees" made out of wire and cloth, and painted "streets"—all in order to mislead any enemy aircraft. (However, during World War II, the U.S. mainland was completely spared from air attacks since the enemy simply did not have aircraft with such range.) The factory buildings had no windows (creating a natural blackout), but were instead air-conditioned and fitted with pleasant, non-blinding lighting on the inside.

Donald Douglas, the owner of Douglas Aircraft Company, had bought 1.5 million square feet of land next to the Daugherty Field airfield (currently the Long Beach Airport) in Long Beach, California, in the summer of 1940, to build a new, gigantic plant for airplane production. Construction was begun immediately, and in September, 1941, the aircraft works were completed, with eleven different factory and office buildings.

Douglas Aircraft Company had developed successful military aircraft such as the A-20 Havoc (which the British called the Boston) and the A-26 Invader. But the one that had given the company its reputation above all else was the commercial aircraft Douglas Commercial, abbreviated DC. With the DC-2, a twin-engine all-metal aircraft that could seat 14 passengers, Douglas showed for the first time that commercial aviation could be both comfortable and safe. This machine, which was presented in 1934, became an immediate success and was bought by airlines all over the world.

The success of the DC-2 led to a follow-up, the DC-3. This was slightly bigger—its length was about the same, but its wingspan was 95 ft 2 in against its predecessor's 85 ft, and on the inside, the passengers' cabin was 92 inches wide, against 66 inches in the DC-2. The number of passenger seats could be expanded to between 21 and 32. In addition, the aircraft was both faster (cruising speed at 207 mph against 174 mph for the DC-2) and had a longer range: it increased from 1,085 to 1,500 miles. The DC-3 came into service in 1936.

This excellent transport aircraft soon caught the U.S. military's attention, and in September, 1940, it placed an order for 147 militarized versions of the DC-3. Douglas modified these aircraft in several areas. Firstly, the crew was expanded from two to four men: Pilot, Co-pilot, Navigator, and Signaler. A two-piece cargo door was installed on the left side of the fuselage, and in order to accommodate a larger payload—6,000 lbs—the floor of the fuselage was reinforced. This meant that the wingspan had to be extended even further, to 95 ft 6 in. Thus, the aircraft's empty weight increased from 16,865 lb to 18,135 lb, and cruising speed dropped to 160 mph, that is, considerably slower than for the civilian version. In order not to increase weight and drag more, it was decided not to add any armament. The military version was designated Carrier-47, abbreviated C-47, and would be dubbed the Skytrain (Dakota by the British). Until the C-47 came into production in January, 1942, 607 DC-3s had been made.

The standard engine in the C-47 was the air-cooled, 14-cylinder Pratt & Whitney R-1830-90C Twin Wasp radial engine with two rows. With 1,200 hp at takeoff, it was stronger than the 9-cylinder Wright R-1820 Cyclone engines that the DC-3 was originally fitted with, but pretty soon, the DC-3 was also fitted with Twin Wasp engines.

In Long Beach, several different aircraft types were made, including 3,000 of the 12,371 four-engine Boeing B-17 Flying Fortresses that were produced during the war, and, in addition, about 2,000 light bombers. But the "queen" of the aircraft in Long Beach was the C-47 Skytrain. Between 1942 and 1945, 10,072 DC-3 fuselages were made, 8,000 of which were the military version C-47. More than half of them, over 4,000, were made in Long Beach.

In early 1942, the U.S. Army Aviation placed a new order for 1,270 C-47s with Douglas Aircraft Company. This was followed by three new orders in quick succession—for 134 in July, 2,000 in September, and 2,000 in December, 1942. The last and largest order was placed with Douglas in Long Beach. One of these two thousand was a model A-60-DL* C-47, USAF order no. 20669, and production number 13883. This individual aircraft left the manufacturing hall

---

* "DL" indicates Douglas, Long Beach. The C-47A was different from the later model C-47B by the latter having modified Twin Wasp engines with two-stage superchargers for better performance at higher altitudes.

40 % of the employees at the Douglas Aircraft Company in Long Beach, California, were women. Pictured here are C-47s under production in Long Beach. (NARA.)

and was delivered to the U.S. Army Aviation on October 5, 1943.[43] Our "Daisy" was born—even though that was a name that she would be given many years after the war. For reasons of simplicity, however, we will choose to call her Daisy anyway from now on.

In the U.S. Air Force, aircraft were not marked with their factory production numbers, but were given their own serial numbers. In Daisy's case, that became 43-30732. This number was typically painted on the tailfin, but in Daisy's case, 330732 was strangely enough painted on her fin.

On October 17, 1943, Daisy was flown to the Baer Army Air Base near the famous Fort Wayne, Indiana.[44] This airbase, which had been named after Paul Baer, a fighter ace in World War One, born in Fort Wayne, was one of several similar establishments used to receive, inspect, and provide supplementary armament for new aircraft. This took place in two phases. During the first, the techni-

U.S. Air Force Record Card for C-47, Serial Number 43-30732, that is, Daisy. (Via Tom Martin.)

cal staff thoroughly scrutinized Daisy to ensure that everything was in order—for example, whether there were any loose electric wires, leaking hydraulics or other fluids, whether the generators were functioning properly, whether all instruments worked, and so on.

During the second phase, trial flights were carried out. The engines were given a trial run, and then, Daisy rolled out and took off. She flew north from Baer, to Kendaville, and then back again, a trip of about 80 miles. During the first stage, the radio and all instruments were checked for proper functioning. Upon approaching Kendaville, the pilot shut down one engine to see how the aircraft behaved, restarted it, and flew back. At the airbase were engineers both from Pratt & Whitney and Douglas, ready to give expert advice.

When Daisy had made it through all the tests, extra fuel tanks were fitted to the fuselage. After 12 hours of trial and transfer flights, she took off on November 12, 1943, on her long flight to North Africa and the U.S. 12th Air Force. On November 20, 1943, she arrived at Marrakesh, and was stationed there as a reserve.[45]

Daisy and Moh fly to England

Meanwhile, life continued at the same calm pace for the men of the 14th Troop Carrier Squadron in Sciacca, Sicily. Norbert Moh, who had been appointed the squadron's sports leader, was tasked with leading a program for physical exercise every day except Sundays between 2 pm and 3 pm. However, the frequent rains this winter often obstructed outdoors sports.

Christmas Day was celebrated by the officers and troops separately. Moh and the other officers had their Christmas dinner at a newly-opened officers' club, and a trio from the men—The Torrid Trio with bass, drums, and saxophone—entertained them with music. In the evening, they watched the movie "The Lady Eve,"* a screwball comedy featuring Henry Fonda and Barbara Stanwyck which, according to the unit diary, aroused much amused laughter.[46]

Early the next morning, the squadron went into formation for an unexpected "flying inspection" by none other than General Mark Clark. Splashing through the soaking mud, the entire squadron marched out to meet the general, who awarded medals and then inspected the quarters. The following night, there was a formation flight exercise.[47]

On December 27, towing gliders was practiced. Moh participated in two such exercises, the first one during daytime. During the other practice flight, at night, Moh was kept from landing by—as the unit diary puts it—"obstacles on the runway." Only after one hour was he able to land his C-47. These practice flights continued every day during the rest of the year.

On December 28, it was noted in the unit diary that Norbert Moh and 2nd Lieutenant Wassil had set up a volleyball net and drawn up a ground just outside the mess, which was received with great enthusiasm.

---

* See Appendix 1, Film Section, Page 103.

A tragic accident took place at the 14th Troop Carrier Squadron the next day, December 29. During a formation takeoff with nine aircraft at 1820 hours, one of the machines (C-47A 42-92067) with the pilot, 2nd Lieutenant William J. Dominick, suddenly veered right at an altitude of only about three meters, striking the control tower antenna with its starboard wing. This threw the aircraft to the side so that it flew into the aircraft 42-23642, where a large hole was torn up in the left side of the fuselage. Exactly what happened next was never made clear, but Dominick's aircraft seems to have tipped over. One of its propellers cut the tail of 42-23635 to pieces, and then, the machine slammed into the starboard wing of the aircraft 42-05684*, crashing into the runway and exploding. The aircraft was ablaze for about 60 seconds before the staff that had come running to the scene was able to quench the flames. The cabin turned out to be completely crushed. When the ambulance arrived, the flight engineer, Sergeant Robert H. Starr, was already dead. The co-pilot, 2nd Lieutenant Jerome V. Graves, died soon after being pulled from the wreckage, and 2nd Lieutenant Dominick died of his serious injuries the following morning. The only survivor was the signaler, Sergeant Howard Walbridge, who escaped with a broken leg and some cuts. He was transported to a hospital in Palermo. The following day, the three dead airmen were buried in the American section of the Ponte Olivo cemetery.[48]

On New Year's Eve, 2nd Lieutenant Moh took up two new pilots, the 2nd Lieutenants Joseph Vrable and Mann, to practice landings. Before being forced to abort because of approaching bad weather, they managed to carry out four landings during the course of one hour.[49]

Then, the New Year celebrations followed, and on January 1, the following note was made in the unit diary, "Roast turkey, All-American symbol for festive, good eating, saluted the Squadron

---

* The aircraft 42-23642 was a complete write-off, and the 42-05684 was first registered as badly damaged, but was never repaired and was scrapped on January 8, 1944.

as the first dinner for 1944. Into the eternal mess kits and into the ever-present metal dinnerware were heaped generous portions of both white and dark meat, as you preferred it.

No man cried 'Not enough'! The Squadron had been filled with a good thing. Some of the Squadron personnel were still not quite right after last night's genial welcome of the New Year now in a position to forget it. The Sicilian weather, however, did seem oblivious to the fact that this was a holiday, the beginning of the world's most important twelve months. The Sicilian weather was in an ugly mood: rainy, cold, and generally miserable. It was open house all day both at the officers and EM's clubs. In the evening the 61st TCG Orchestra played to a packed house of mixed personnel at the officer's [sic] club. The renowned bar was wide open, refreshments gratis to all comers. The program presented overflowed with songs new and nostalgically ancient, old fashioned folk music, and the very latest swing. Waggish F/O Albertto F. Perna did the chore as Master of Ceremonies."

On January 17, the squadron received a very welcome former member, Major Lewis S. Frederick—the infinitely popular squadron commander, who had left the unit in June, 1943, to become a liaison officer at the wing. In the squadron diary, it was noted, "The Squadron rejoiced because Major 'Freddie' and his dog Jerry had always been high in his estimation." Lewis himself said that the 14th Troop Carrier Squadron was his favorite unit in the entire group, it was "his life" and everything he did was "for the best of the squadron." He had the entire staff of the squadron stand in formation and said that everyone in the unit, regardless of military rank, was welcome to his tent to tell him of any problems they might have.

On January 18, all men in the unit were summoned to an exhibition of British coins and notes in order to familiarize themselves with them—something that clarified which of the camp rumors that turned out to be true. After that, the navigators and signalmen from the unit were taught by officers from the Royal Air Force which navigational aids that existed in England. Meanwhile, the pilots learned the British airfields' specific landing procedures. In connection with this, a strict ban on visiting Sciacca was introduced for all personnel.

The lack of female companionship made many in the unit irritable. On February 10, they saw the movie "Higher and Higher"* starring Frank Sinatra and the 23-year-old Frenchwoman Michèle Morgan (it was Sinatra's debut movie). The squadron diary commented, "The men in the 61st TCG decided that they did not care for Frank Sinatra's swoon singing at the 61st TCG theater tonight, Sinatra's efforts were shouted down. The basic reason for such utter distaste is envy. The men are a bit jealous of Sinatra's feminine following back in the States."

On February 12, an order was given that all aircraft in the squadron were to fly to the el-Aouina airbase at Tunis and land there. That was the first step of regrouping. In el-Aouina, the officers were quartered in houses, which was very welcome, especially as temperatures dropped just below 32°F at night and the weather shifted between rain and sleet.[50]

They stayed for two days in Tunis, and on the 15th at 0730 hours, the aircraft took off again. This time, the flight went westward. Moh recounted this flight, "In spite of us giving full throttle and trying to climb, we dropped by 500 feet per minute. We'd ended up in the strong downwinds sweeping along the eastern side of the Atlas Mountains. But by turning 90 degrees, we were able to climb again."[51] After more

---

* See Appendix 1, Film section, Page 103.

** 41-18384 was also made in Long Beach. The aircraft's documentation shows that it was handed over to the U.S. Army Aviation on June 2, 1942, and was flown to North Africa on May 7, 1943. On June 26, 1945, it returned to the U.S., and was handed over on November 19 to the Reconstruction Finance Corporation (RFC), the American armed forces' division for liquidating surplus equipment after the war. The aircraft was leased in May, 1947, by the American airline Pioneer Air Lines, and flew under civil registration as NC47996 under the moniker "Ben Milan" on commercial routes, mainly between the U.S. and Mexico. On March 11, 1952, the aircraft was recalled by the U.S. Air Force, and was given the designation C-117C there. On October 13, 1953, the aircraft crashed with Edward E. Lane as its pilot at the Mitchell Air Force Base. However, it was registered as mothballed in September, 1955, and has subsequently probably been scrapped.

Wrecks of German Junkers 52 transport aircraft and one Junkers 87 Stuka at the el-Aouina airbase at Tunis. (NARA.)

than seven hours' flying, they landed in Marrakesh—where they were again quartered in tents.

Here, Moh had to hand over his old aircraft (41-18384**) to a newcomer to the squadron, and, instead, was given a new aircraft, with the number 330732 on its tailfin—our Daisy.[52] It was the replacement for one of the aircraft that had been a casualty of December 29. Daisy was painted olive drab on top and on the sides, with the serial number in yellow on its tailfin. The underside of the fuselage was light gray. 1st Lieutenant Moh was by then a very experienced C-47 pilot. He had carried out 161 flights totaling 315 flight hours in the aircraft type.[53]

Four large 100-gallon fuel tanks were stowed in and secured in Daisy's cargo hold, and were connected to the engines for the long

47

flight that would take her to England. There, blue formation lights were fitted onto the wingtips, so as to facilitate night flights, and armor was attached underneath the pilots' seats. Moh and the other pilots were awoken at 0200 hours in the morning of February 16 and were ordered to be ready for takeoff in their aircraft by 0300 hours. On their way there, they were given a box with sandwiches and oranges. But just as Moh had sat down in Daisy's pilot seat, a counterorder was issued: The flight has been postponed. So, instead of a tough long-haul flight, he and his comrades had a day off, which many spent catching up on lost sleep. At 1600 hours, it was announced that everybody was to be ready for takeoff at some point during the following night.[54]

At 0200 hours on February 17, the call came once again. After breakfast, the pilots, navigators, and signalmen gathered for orders between 0300 and 0400 hours. They were briefed that all aircraft in the 14th Carrier Squadron were to take off beginning at 0515 hours, with two minutes' interval, and that the destination was the British Isles. They were to be part of a formation of about 250 aircraft of various sizes. The first leg of the flight would be heading 330 degrees, until reaching the 10th meridian west. The 10th meridian west, which crosses the Atlantic just west of Portugal and the southwest tip of Ireland, was to be followed until reaching 50 degrees north, and from there, the aircraft were to turn to heading 60 degrees towards Valley in Wales, where they were to land. Since the Germans controlled France and had plenty of agents in the neutral countries of Spain and Portugal, they had to avoid flying over these countries. The airmen could expect overcast over the Bay of Biscay, and were instructed to fly at an altitude so that they had the clouds beneath them. On their way towards the aircraft, sandwich packages were handed out again.[55]

Once again, Norbert Moh sat in Daisy's pilot seat. Next to him, one of the co-pilots was seated. The regular co-pilot in Moh's crew was 2nd Lieutenant Ernest M. Martzen, but on this flight, Moh had three other airmen as co-pilots and backup pilots—the 2nd

Lieutenants Charles W. Adamson, Peter Lawrence Bruno, and Milton Stanley Cohen. His regular flight engineer and signaler respectively, Sergeants William H. Gray and Arvid J. Blomdal, were onboard, however.[56] With a U.S Air Force term, Gray was called Crew Chief—which can be misleading, as the pilot always was the chief of the crew. Instead, a Crew Chief was the designation of the flight engineer who "owned" an aircraft—he knew his individual aircraft back to front, and it was always him (the same man) who was onboard during every flight. Pilots could be substituted, but the Crew Chief should always be the same.

Edsel Clayton Linn was appointed navigator for this flight. In addition, 2nd Lieutenant Peter L. Bruno and Sergeants Louis Raymond Janek and Andrew Theodore Fehl came along as well.[57]

Just before takeoff, there was a radio message from the control tower in Marrakesh that the crews were to aim for St. Mawgan in Cornwall (the peninsula in southwestern England) instead of Valley. The signalers were instructed to tune their radios to the emergency frequency.

Having been flying in a loose formation over the dark sea for several hours, daylight started breaking, and then, the men aboard Daisy could discern the Portuguese coast to their right. They guessed that the brightly lit city that they saw was Lisbon. A sudden and quite strong westerly wind raised the demands on the pilots to stay on course. Once out above the Bay of Biscay, they flew above the reported overcast, and only had a glimpse of the Atlantic every now and then through the odd break in the clouds. As the aircraft was approaching the British Isles, the signaler contacted a radio station in Plymouth to check their position. The pilots were also helped over the radio by air traffic controllers on the ground. Half an hour before reaching England, they flew into dense fog. They did not know it at the time—but they would not see the sun again for a whole week.

All except four of the squadron's aircraft landed at the British military airbase in St. Mawgan at around 1700 hours. The four missing aircraft had gotten lost, but landed in St. Mawgan the following day.

Thus, the 14th Troop Carrier Squadron had managed to carry out the dangerous transit flight—past the German-occupied France—completely without any losses.[58]

When Daisy had landed, the cargo hatch was opened—the British winter chill immediately penetrated the aircraft as a reminder of what lay ahead—and a British sergeant called out to the crew to stay aboard for two minutes while the plane was sprayed with insect poison. Then, Moh and the signaler were shown to the briefing room, where they gave their report and handed over all of their maps and other North Africa-related documents that they had brought from Marrakesh. After breakfast consisting of cornflakes and milk, all underwent medical examination.

After that, it was time for new orders. Each crew was given a set of maps over England. They would soon take off again and fly to the airfield that would become the unit's base for more than one year, Barkston Heath. During the 250-mile flight to Barkston Heath, Moh could observe that England looked like a single great golf course with lots of airfields from the air.

The airbase — Barkston Heath

The airfield Barkston Heath, 80 miles east-south-east of Liverpool and about 90 miles north-northwest of London, is located in the middle of the English countryside in Lincolnshire. It is described in the following way, "The terrain around Barkston Heath Royal Air Force Base is mainly flat. Barkston Heath Royal Air Force Base is located on a height running from north to south. The highest point in the vicinity is 436 feet above sea level, 1.2 miles southwest of Barkston Heath Royal Air Force Base. The area around Barkston Heath Royal Air Force Base is quite densely populated, with 139 inhabitants per square kilometer. The nearest large town is Grantham, 5 miles southwest of Barkston Heath Royal Air Force Base. The area around Barkston Heath Royal Air Force Base is mainly farm land."[59]

On Barkston Heath, a grass airfield was created in the 1930s as an emergency landing strip for the bugger airbase of Cranwell, situated more than three miles further north.

In the summer of 1943, work was begun to expand Barkston Heath into a bigger base for bombers, which meant constructing three paved runways, one apron with space for 50 large aircraft, seven hangars (one B1-type so-called "double hangar" and six ordinary T2 hangars). The runways were 150 feet wide and between 4,200 and 6,000 ft long. On all sides of them, there were grassy fields. Barkston Heath is still being used, and the old control tower also remains. In January, 1944, Barkston Heath was taken over by the IX. Transport Aviation Command of the American 9th Air Force—which the 61st Troop Carrier Group and the 52nd Troop Carrier Wing were now subordinated to—and was designated Station 483.

As the 72 C-47s came roaring in across Grantham during their approach to land at Barkston Heath on Friday, February 18, 1944, the townspeople were standing and watching in awe. One of them was a 19-year-old girl named Margaret Roberts, who was working in the family's grocery store. After the war, she would embark on a political career and eventually became British Prime Minister. But by then, she had married and had taken the surname Thatcher…

2nd Lieutenant James F. Shemas of the 14th TCS recounted, "The planes were given dispersal areas. The unloading of the planes has not started yet. The officers and men have simply been lingering around the barracks, eating and sleeping, and marveling at the frequency with which steak is being served in the mess hall."[60] There was a lack of coal, and because of rationing, it was only permitted to light a fire between 5 pm and 10 pm.

The Americans suffered severely from the cold, which penetrated everywhere, and everybody agreed that even though they had been staying in tents in Sciacca, they had not been as cold there. Captain Augustine T. S. Stoney recounted that he spent the entire day of February 19 trying to keep warm by walking briskly between the various mess halls and office buildings. On February 20, the engineers took out all the Bolero tanks from the aircraft. The first few days in Barkston Heath, the men slept in the mess halls, but on February 22, they moved into the newly erected Quonset Huts, provisional metal barracks.[61]

One of the pilots of the 61st Troop Carrier Group, Charles N. Fay, wrote in his diary, "It took us several hours to find where we would billet, to get our things to the barracks where we would live. Our barracks, were niessen [sic] huts, and located in a tree belt, about three miles from the line. We had to go around several farm houses to get to our billet, and the narrow English road curled like a snake. All of the roads, in England, are paved, but none of them are much larger, or wider than a lane and they are all derived from paths, and the cow lanes, so driving in Limeland is a real headache, with side-swiping another car, a common thing.

The runways were real large affairs, and were of concrete, with a tar substance, covering the concrete, and a non-skid concoction mixed with the tar. The non-skid was large slivers of wood, that were

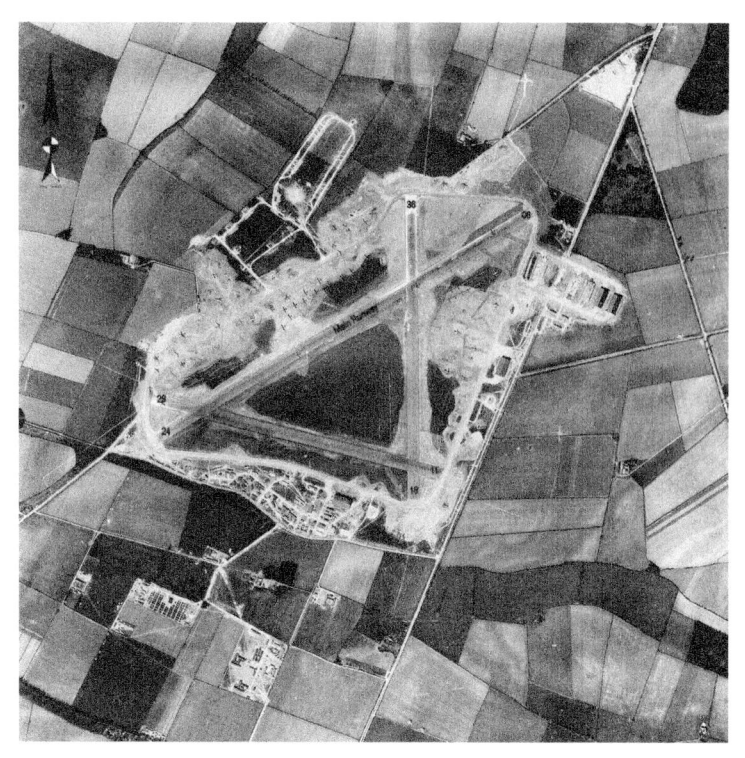

Air photo of the Barkston Heath base. (NARA.)

mixed with the tar. The perimeter, around the field was the same as the runways, with parking areas, shooting off from it. Every once in a while, a camouflage outfit, would come around and spray a paint, over the runways and other strips, the same color as the surrounding ground. (. . .)

All of the windows had special blackout curtains, and as soon as the sun had set, the curtains, had to be properly drawn. All doors had special, double openings, so no light could be seen, when they were opened. Walking around at night, was like being blind, and it was a happy night, when there was a full moon, so that one could see where they were going. All of the vehicles had special blackout lights and you couldn't see one, at night, until it was right up on you."[62]

The reason why the 52nd Troop Carrier Wing, including the 61st TCG, was moved to England, was that it was to participate in the invasion of Normandy that had been planned for a long time. 1st Lieutenant Clark O. Thornton recounts the early days at Barkston Heath, "We were kept quite busy flying cargo and people within England, and conducting various kinds of practice missions. So we became fairly familiar with places in England, Scotland and Northern Ireland."[63]

Due to bad weather, it initially took a few days before the first flights could be made. But Thursday, February 24, dawned with brilliant sunshine. Moh and Daisy took off together with eight other aircraft on a first practice flight that lasted for two hours above the British landscape.

Then, the bad weather returned, again preventing all flying. Instead, the men could go to Grantham.

Outside the huts at Barkston Heath in the spring of 1944. (Photo: Norbert Moh. Via Cheryl Moh Grau.)

In the 14th Squadron's diary, it was noted, "In comparison with those of Africa or Sicily, English towns are excellent. Contrary to popular belief, English beer is a good beer. Scotch is scarce, is rationed, and comes in once a week. It's sold within 15 minutes after being put on sale. The fact that the English girls speak the same language makes them a bit more interesting than the French or Italian girls. So runs the general consensus." Grantham was not only an ancient medieval trading town, but also the place where the inhabitants of the surrounding countryside came for entertainment during the weekends. For that reason, it had an unusual number of pubs and other entertainment venues for its quite modest size, little over 20,000 inhabitants. Among the most popular venues were the Empire Theatre and the Victorian dance hall, the Guildhall, with room for 200 guests. As a curiosity, it could be mentioned that Grantham in 1915 became the first town in the world to hire a female police officer, Mrs. Edith Smith, who today is an important person in the town's history.

Another thing that made Grantham stand out was that its Member of Parliament, Denis Kendall, was a member of the right-wing extremist and anti-Semitic British National Party, which had emerged out of the British Union of Fascists. Kendall was the head of the government-financed arms factory Manufacture And Research Co (BMARC). Because of his right-wing extremist opinions, he soon attracted the attention of the British Intelligence, and they even secretly managed to recruit his wife, Virginia. The Security Service, MI5, expressed great concern that he carelessly revealed the war industry's production figures during his election speeches. But the inhabitants of Grantham elected him in 1942, and he was reelected several times and was an MP until 1950. Amongst other things, he gained popularity by criticizing what he called "the gang" around Winston Churchill. The arrival of American air soldiers at Barkston Heath was something that this full-fledged populist would exploit to the full to his own advantage—more on that later.

On Sunday, February 26, there was a heavy snowfall, making every sortie unthinkable. One of the squadron's captains, Arnold Newman, slipped and broke an arm. But it was important that the unit was well prepared for the forthcoming great mission, so the 61st TCG's C-47s flew as soon as the weather permitted.

In March, three training flights with parachute drops were carried out, two of them by night, with British paratroopers and Americans from the 508th PIR of the 82nd U.S. Airborne Division.[64] On March 3, Daisy flew for four hours, out of which Moh was in control for two, and the co-pilot, 2nd Lieutenant Ernest Martzen, for two, landing three times.[65] The high pressure remained, with dropping temperatures as a consequence. On March 4, it was so cold that the gasoline in the pipes of some of the squadron's aircraft started thickening, meaning that they could not start. But Daisy made it up in the air with Moh, and flew for one hour and fifteen minutes, with two landings. On March 5, they flew for a new training lasting three hours and fifteen minutes.[66]

It is possible that Daisy was struck by some kind of technical fault, because while other aircraft were up in the sky on March 6, she remained on the ground, and Moh's flight log shows that he took her up for 20 minutes on the 7th.[67] Then, yet another few days with poor flying weather followed, when time was instead spent on theoretical education, including a lecture by two British officers on radio procedure in England. In spite of heavy winds on March 11, it was decided to take advantage of the reasonably clearing weather for new practice flights.[68] Daisy and Moh were up together with none other machines from the squadron. The aircraft swayed considerably in the wind, making some of the crew members—albeit none of the pilots—airsick. Daisy was up for three hours and fifteen minutes. Moh and Martzen took the controls half of the time each.[69]

On March 16, the next flight with Daisy was carried out, and Moh and Martzen took turns in control.[70] The next day, underbelly racks for supply canisters with parachutes were fitted to the fuselages of the unit's C-47s, meaning that no flights took place. On March 18, the ground crew of the 14th Squadron finally arrived after a long sea voyage with the old passenger liner *Capetown Castle* from Sicily to Liverpool. Two days later, the men arrived at Barkston Heath.[71]

On March 19, the next training flight was carried out during daytime, and in the evening, Moh rolled out the machine onto the runway for a night-flight exercise, when suddenly the air raid alarm went off. The flight had to be aborted.[72] Soon afterwards, there was a distant rumble of exploding bombs from the Hull direction, and to the north, the night sky flared up every now and then. 131 German bombers had been sent in against the British port town of Hull, forty miles north of Barkston Heath. The operation was a complete failure from the German point of view: All bombs fell over the countryside or in the sea—in the city itself, the inhabitants did not even know that their town was the Luftwaffe's target that night. Nine German bombers did not return to their bases afterwards.[73]

The 14th Squadron's diary for March 20, 1944, reads, "The weather was rainy, miserable and the roads were sloppy with mud, none of which prevented officers and EM of the organization from trying out their new English bicycles. Squadron supply received a

The mess hall at Barkston Heath. (Photo: Norbert Moh. Via Cheryl Moh Grau.)

shipment of 25 bikes and distributed them among those members of the ground echelon who were entitled to them. Major Lewis S. Frederick held a staff meeting to discuss military conduct for the Squadron on the post."

Before noon next day, pilots, navigators, paratrooper officers, and jump masters were summoned to the wing headquarters, where they were briefed about a jump exercise that was to be carried out at 0200 hours the following night. A few hours later, it was announced that the exercise had been postponed to the following day.[74] Moh took one and Martzen one flight with Daisy during daytime of March 22. At the last one, paratroopers did an exercise jump. At 0830-1030 hours on March 23, Moh flew with Daisy in an exercise where take-off and landing in formation was carried out.[75]

It was not only bad weather that prevented flights, but sometimes—for example, on March 26—it was because the British airspace simply was full of training aircraft. More than ten thousand aircraft were stationed in England, and as soon as the weather permitted, the units tried to practice as much as possible in the air ahead of the forthcoming invasion of Normandy. Therefore, they had to take the chance as soon as there was a window of opportunity. At 1100 hours in March 27, the crews of the 14th TCS were told that they were to take off with paratroopers immediately after lunch, so they quickly gulped down their food and went to the aircraft where the paratroopers were waiting. At 1307 hours, Daisy rolled out onto the runway and took off with the soldiers onboard.[76] These jumped just above the intended drop zone, which the air crew was much commended for. On this flight, Moh was the pilot in control of Daisy all the time.[77]

A winch for towing gliders was fitted onto Daisy, and the next day, Moh and Martzen practiced towing a Horsa glider with her. On the 29th, a day with drizzle, Daisy was only up for fifteen minutes with Martzen in control.[78]

A major exercise called "Sidecar" was to be carried out on April 1, but it had to be postponed because of bad weather, which remained

In front of Daisy at Barkston Heath at the end of April, 1944: From the left: Norbert Moh, Charles W. Adamson, William H. Gray, and Arvid J. Blomdal. At this time, Daisy carries mission markings for three goods transport flights in England (symbolized by the train, followed by as many strokes as completed missions of that kind) and two medical flights (symbolized by a Red Cross mark and two strokes) — see the adjacent images. These markings symbolize the flights on April 10 to the Lanford Lodge military airbase near Belfast, on April 15 to Shipsham, on April 23 to Bottesford, and on April 24 and 27 1944 to Cottesmore. Note the tactical marking "104" on the nose. (Photo: Via Blomdal family.)

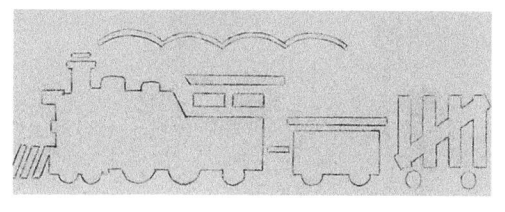

for a few days.[79] On April 3, the unit was alerted that there would be an inspection by two generals the following day. Indeed, Major General Ralph Royce, assisting commander of the Allied Invasion Force, and the commander of the 52nd Troop Carrier Wing, Harold L. Clark, who had been promoted to Brigadier General, did turn up. The purpose of their visit was to make an inspection ahead of "Sidecar," which was to be carried out that night. But the best news for many of the men at Barkston Heath on April 4 was the arrival of twenty-five female nurses who had been stationed at the base.[80]

At 2330 hours on April 5, all of the squadron's twelve aircraft took off for the sizeable exercise together with a large number of aircraft from other units. Daisy participated in "Sidecar-Mercator," which meant that she dropped paratroopers. At 0310 hours, all of the squadron's aircraft had landed again.[81]

An evaluation of this exercise showed that it had ended in total chaos with far too many aircraft at any one time over the drop zone—there was much room for improvement in the procedures.[82] The 14th Troop Carrier Squadron, however, had succeeded better than most of the participating air units—Daisy and nine other aircraft had dropped their paratroopers at the designated points. Only three of the unit's aircraft had failed dropping the paratroopers because of the congestion in the sky above the drop zone.[83]

The next time that Daisy flew was April 10, when she transported cargo to the British military airbase Lanford Lodge near Belfast. The following day, she and Moh participated in an exercise concerning towing gliders in a formation.[84]

After the landing, the crews were reached by an order that prohibited them from leaving the airbase from midnight and until 1200 hours on Friday, April 14. The reason was that the entire 61st Group was carrying out a new exercise on April 13-14.[85] On both of these days, Daisy and nine other C-47s from the 14th Squadron flew down to Greenham Common, where they picked up gliders that they towed back to Barkston Heath. As far as can be judged, someone else than Moh was the pilot of Daisy during this exercise, since there is no corresponding note in Moh's pilot logbook. It has not been possible to establish who it was. The same goes for April 15, when the war diary for the 14th TCS shows that Daisy flew twice—once for a transport to Shipsham, and once for an exercise in towing gliders in a formation.

In the morning of April 18, there was a magnificent show in the air above Barkston Heath, as large numbers of Flying Fortresses returned from a bomb raid against Germany. They had taken part in the great attack with 776 deployed bombers against German aircraft industries southwest of Berlin. Nineteen bombers had been lost, and no less

Daisy and the other C-47s of the 14th Troop Carrier Squadron before takeoff from Barkston Heath. (NARA.)

than 204 were damaged. One of the bombers began circling over the airfield, and then deployed its undercarriage and landed. Immediately, a rumor started spreading that the aircraft had been badly damaged in combat, and had ten wounded onboard, but in reality, it had landed for a planned visit.[86] A few hours later, Daisy participated in a formation flight exercise, now with Moh as her pilot again.[87]

The following day, the same scenes played out over Barkston Heath, when a seemingly never-ending number of large four-engine bombers passed by after a new raid against Germany. The men at the airfield were cheering and waving at the bombers and told each other that they really were giving Hitler hell. This operation, too, which involved 772 bombers, had been aimed at German aircraft factories.

On April 20, Moh practiced landing with gliders with Daisy, and carried out three of them at Barkston Heath.[88] After the last few weeks' training, the time was considered to have come to repeat the previously failed exercise, now under the code name "Mush." In the morning of April 21, the air crews were awoken already at 0200 hours, and after breakfast, they went straight to their aircraft—one of them being Daisy[89]—where British paratroopers sat waiting. At 0502 hours, the 14th TCS started taking off. At 0641 hours, its aircraft rumbled in over Drop Zone "Z," at the exact designated time and in perfect formation. All paratroopers were dropped just above the zone. Afterwards, the higher headquarters commended the squadron for the excellent carrying out of the mission.[90]

Following a new training flight lasting two hours and thirty-five minutes with Moh in control on April 22, Daisy was used for a transport to Bottesford on April 23, and on the 24th and 27th, Moh flew her for a transport mission to Cottesmore and back. On April 28, Moh again practiced towing gliders with Daisy, and on April 29, she was flown by Martzen during a formation flight exercise together with a large number of other aircraft.[91] That evening, there was a dance at the base for the officers, with women who had been invited from Grantham and who were fetched by the unit's trucks.[92]

There was a special reason for this event being held at the base rather than the men going to the entertainment metropolis of Grantham; there, some of the inhabitants had begun complaining about the large numbers of foreign flying soldiers, whom they felt were flooding the city. This discontent was cunningly exploited by Denis Kendall, the city's right-wing extremist MP, who announced that he had sent a report on the state of things to the Home Secretary Herbert Morrison calling for immediate action. The fact that this was wildly exaggerated is made clear by the head of the Grantham police declaring that he had no complaints about the American soldiers' conduct.

Home Secretary Morrison responded, following an investigation, to Kendall's petition to the Parliament, saying that it "gave neither a fair nor accurate picture of the position." Kendall, who was supported by many of the town clergy, then answered in a classic manner that it was "unfit for a woman" of Grantham "to walk unescorted through the town at night or in the daytime" because of the many foreign soldiers. However, many in town believed that this was not true at all. The Rev. John Barrett of Fuller Baptist Church in Grantham, for example, wrote in the church magazine that "it is not only Americans who accost girls and women in Kettering and elsewhere. It is also unfortunately true that girls and women sometimes take their share in accosting."[93] One of the townspeople, Terry Roberts, remembered that Grantham High Street during the war became known for having a "five bob" side, where officers picked up women, and a "half-crown" side*, for non-commissioned officers and troops. The nineteen-year-old Margaret Roberts's (later Thatcher) letters to a friend about dances in the area during the war always mention the "hordes of flight lieutenants eager for a dance."[94]

---

* Five Bob was slang for five shillings. The half-crown coin was the equivalent of a little more than half of this value—two shillings and sixpence, or one eighth of a pound. The amounts corresponded to about 21 U.S. cents and 53 U.S. cents respectively in those days.

Kendall also complained that the Americans were allowed to book the large Guildhall, something he claimed that British soldiers had not been permitted to do.[95] Even though this was not consistent with reality either, the 14th Squadron's diary noted that the Guildhall was closed to officers from the airbase this particular Saturday. Kendall would continue making things difficult for the American airmen for quite some time.

Apparently, however, neither air officers nor many of the town's young ladies let themselves be deterred by that on this particular Saturday. The Squadron diary commented, "The dance was a success, the drinks were abundant." The next day, the men were given leave, and took advantage of the sunny spring weather to take bicycle rides in the surrounding and very beautiful British landscape. The pubs in the surrounding villages were also the objects of many an excursion from Barkston Heath. "Every little hamlet, had several pubs, and this was about the only recreation there was."[96]

On May 5, Moh flew Daisy as the entire squadron contributed to an exercise with 54 aircraft in formation flight.[97] Led by Major Frederick, all aircraft came rumbling in tight formation over the target—which only so happened to be the Guildhall![98]

Six days later, Operation "Eagle" was carried out, which was the dress rehearsal for the great invasion. Both the American airborne divisions and three troop carrier groups were to participate. The day before, the paratroopers from the 82nd Airborne Division arrived at Barkston Heath. At 2200 hours on May 11, Colonel Mitchell, commander of the 61st Troop Carrier Group, gathered all airmen for orders, and at 2350 hours, the aircraft started taking off. In total, 369 aircraft from the 52nd Troop Carrier Wing participated, carrying the 82nd Airborne Division in gliders, and 432 aircraft from the 50th and 53rd Troop Carrier Wings with the 101st Airborne Division. The air route was 250 miles long, half of which being over the sea, and the air crews navigated using the same kinds of light and radar aids that were to be used during the invasion.[99]

Moh's pilot logbook shows that he landed Daisy after five hours' night flight. Since they were not to be debriefed until at 0500 hours, the airmen had a few hours' well-needed sleep after their landings.

During the evaluation, Major General Lewis H. Brereton, commander of U.S. 9th Air Force, which the air transport units belonged to, concluded that "the dress rehearsal indicated to my satisfaction that the plan of employment is practicable from a flight and navigational point of view, and that we have reached an effective state of readiness to carry out the plan."[100] Colonel Mitchell wrote, "It is also obvious to anyone who understands troop-carrier operations where the invasion will be, and looks as if we might get away with it in fairly good shape."[101]

William H. Gray and Arvid J. Blomdal in front of Daisy at Barkston Heath in the spring of 1944. (Photo: Via Blomdal family.)

On May 12, Moh made a two-hour training flight with two landings with Daisy. She seems to have been serviced in some way on the 15th, since all other aircraft in the squadron—one of them with Moh at the controls—did practice flights that day. On May 16, she was back up in the air, this time with a new glider towing exercise with Moh in the left pilot's seat. The next day, Moh took her for a return flight to Base 559, The American Army Aviation's code name for the airfield at Grove, 55 miles west-north-west of London, to carry personnel. On May 22, Moh practiced landings with gliders with Daisy and carried out five landings.[102]

On May 23, it was time for an exercise in evacuating ground units. The unit diary reads, "14th TCS personnel and planes showed how it was done in a demonstration evacuation mission this afternoon. At 1200 they took off to Fairford, which is 20 miles west of Oxford. Corporal William H. Leary, Squadron Public Relations NCO, went along, but not just for the ride. He had a photographer with him making pictures of the event." Moh logged four landings with Daisy and total air time of three hours and five minutes.[103] On May 26, Daisy was used for a personnel transport to Base 489, the airfield at Cottesmore, where the 316th Troop Carrier Group, which was part of the 52nd Troop Carrier Wing, was deployed. The next day, Moh flew her in an exercise in flying in supplies to ground units; no less than seven landings were made in two hours and fifteen minutes.[104]

In the absence of orders for exercises on May 28, the men of the 14th TCS took advantage of the sunny and warm Sunday for long bicycle rides in the surrounding countryside. The next morning, as they came out of their barracks, they were surprised to see the ground being strewed with hundreds, thousands of strips of tinfoil.[105] These had been dropped by German Messerschmitt 410s in order to blind the British radar as they were attacking airbases in the Cambridge area.

During a parachuting exercise on May 30, Moh landed Daisy a full nine times to take paratroopers aboard.[106]

C-47s from the 14th Troop Carrier Squadron with Waco gliders. (AFHRA B0158.)

By early June, it was becoming obvious to the men at Barkston Heath that the great operation was imminent. They were forbidden to leave the base and were alerted to extensive inspection. On June 3, all intelligence officers were summoned to the wing's command post, and they remained there all day while sentries ensured that no-one else could "so much as sniff at the place," as the squadron's diary put it. The next day was spent on theoretical education, and as the airmen came out from the halls, they were surprised to see that their aircraft's wings and fuselages had been painted in black and white zebra stripes. Since they were painted by and, they were not always very even, but they were good enough as marks of identification ahead of the invasion of Normandy.

The operation was in the air as not being very far away, but the terrible weather made it obvious that it would at least not be the following night. In fact, the invasion had been planned to commence during the night of June 4, but due to the weather—low clouds that would make it difficult for the air crews to navigate correctly, and strong winds that created high seas in the English Channel, which would make it impossible to deploy the landing boats—there was a last-minute decision to postpone it all by 24 hours.

At 2030 hours on June 5, the air crews started pouring into the briefing room, where they had been summoned for orders at 2100 hours. There, they remained standing and waiting in small groups, smoking, talking, and laughing, curious as to what they would hear.

At first, the men were instructed to help themselves to equipment that had been placed neatly on a few tables. Moh and the other First Pilots picked up escape accessories and small purses with French currency for each man in their crews from a table. The navigators were given maps with course details. The signalers were given small thin sheets of rice paper, onto which the secret liaison information had been typed. The reason for using rice paper was so that they could be swallowed if necessary, in case the aircraft had to make an emergency landing in hostile territory.[107]

Then, the meeting began. First of all, Captain Arnold Newman ordered everyone to empty their pockets so that nothing could be used by hostile intelligence in case they were shot down. Each man was given a large envelope in which he put his watch, pocketbook, rings, photographs, and so on. After that, he wrote his name on the envelope, and handed it over.

"What about your dog tags? Do you have them?" Newman asked.—"Oh, hell! I left mine in my barracks. How much time do I have?" It was 2nd Lieutenant Erwin Milling, looking absolutely terrified.—"Ten—no, nine—minutes," Newman answered.—"Got a jeep out there?"—"Yeah", Newman answered, turning to the jeep driver, "Okay, run this officer up to his area please." The jeep was off to a flying start and was soon back again. "Did you get your tags?"—"Yes, thanks a lot."[108]

"Suddenly," the 14th Squadron's 1st Lieutenant James Shemas recounted, "Major Lewis S. Frederick was standing atop one of the intelligence's map boxes. It was the usual Major Frederick, calm, cool, collected, enthusiastic and confident in his squadron's ability. It wasn't going to be as hard as you might expect. They've been planning this night for two years and it's going to come off in fine fashion. His few words delivered in an easy going, very much matter-of-fact manner relaxed the tense seriousness which had settled in a few of the men. If there was no extreme, exaggerated joviality, there certainly was no evidence of doubt or nervousness. There was confidence. Confidence: the men wore no impregnated clothing. Confidence: they wore no steel helmets or leggings. Confidence: 'I'll pick up my wallet when I get back.' Confidence: 'Make sure you save some of that chow for me.' Confidence: a group of men about to start on the greatest military operation in history dressed and looking as though they were merely to fly formation over the local area."[109]

Then, the time was 2100 hours: Time for orders. Military police were posted at the doors so that nobody who did not have clearance would be able to enter. Colonel Willis W. Mitchell, Lieutenant Colonel Leo N. O'Connor (operations officer of the 61st Group), and

Flight exercise above the English landscape. One of the aircraft in the picture is Daisy, with Norbert Moh in control. (Photo: Norbert Moh. Via Cheryl Moh Grau.)

Captain Richard E. Scharf (Chief Navigator of the Group) repeated what these 72 crews had heard during the previous day's briefing: Startup of engines at 2315 hours, taxiing onto the runway starting at 2322 hours, takeoff at 2352 hours, assembly in formation over G.D.P. (Barkston Heath) at 0009 hours.[110] Major John E. Gillum (commander of the base defense) gave an updated situation report and read them a rugged but inspiring Order of the Day from Major General Harold Clark. Someone else gave instructions on how to handle any paratroopers who came back with them. One Lieutenant Colonel from the paratroopers loudly exclaimed, "You won't bring any back tonight," which provided some comic relief. "Let's get those troopers into France tonight."[111] The briefing was over.

The airmen were eager. Even though it was some time before they were to be at their aircraft, they chose to go there straight away. They walked around their aircraft, carefully caressing them and controlling that everything was in order. Just before midnight on June 6, 1944, D-Day, the aircraft were lined up three by three in neat V formations and then began rolling out onto the runway. The first one for takeoff was Colonel Mitchell's aircraft 43-30647. The great invasion had begun.

Arnhem

Out of 72 aircraft of the 61st Troop Carrier Group, only one was lost during D-Day, June 6, 1944, but 27 were hit and damaged by the German flak. Daisy was probably one of them, since she did not fly again until June 9, and then for a test flight—in spite of the entire wing being deployed to fly in supplies to the landed airborne units during the night between June 6 and June 7.[112]

When Daisy was operational again, the airborne part of the invasion of Normandy was already over, and the men were now asking themselves what to do. The unit diary for June 13 reads, "The hot talk today but not at all objectionable. Troop Carrier is to be split wide open. Why? Because there's no apparent need for the great number of transports they've got over here. The missions have been completed—they're no further use to us. What about air evacuation? Well, you can see for yourself that the ATC* is taking care of that. Really? Then what's going to become of the 14th TCS and 61st TCG? They'll be left intact and sent back to the States for training in other kinds of operational aircraft. What kind? Maybe C-54's, B-26's, and B-29's [sic]."**

There was not much flying during the rest of the month. On June 19, Daisy was used for personnel transports to Base 186 and back. The next day, Moh flew her on personnel transport to something noted as a "secret destination"; it must have been quite a remote location, as the flight took five hours and five minutes and inclu-

---

* The U.S. Air Transport Command (ATC) was established in 1942 with commercial aircraft and staff from civilian airlines. Its original mission was to transport aircraft from the U.S. to Europe, but after the invasion of Normandy, it was also used for transport missions to the units on the continent.

** Douglas C-54 Skymaster was a four-engine transport plane that was the backbone of the air transport command, and its uses included transport flights across the Atlantic. The civilian version was called DC-4. Martin B-26 Marauder was a twin-engine medium bomber. Boeing B-29 Superfortress was a four-engine heavy bomber, which was exclusively deployed against Japan during World War II.

Three C-47s from the 14th Troop Carrier Squadron, having landed at an airfield in France. (Photo: Norbert Moh. Via Cheryl Moh Grau.)

ded three landings. Two days later, Daisy flew personnel to Base 466, Membury, about sixty miles west-south-west of London, where the 436th Troop Carrier Group was stationed.[113]

Eventually, the officers of the unit started worrying that the good state of alert would be impaired by all inactivity. At a meeting, they decided that exercise activities would be resumed, in spite of missions for the unit. Norbert Moh and 1st Lieutenant William Metcalf were appointed air training leaders.[114] The training flights began again on June 27, when Moh and Ernest Martzen flew Daisy during an exercise in dropping supplies for airborne units. On June 28, Moh performed five practice landings with Daisy for two hours and twenty-five minutes, and the next day, there were seven similar landings.[115]

The month of July began with a torrential rainstorm, preventing all flying. But in spite of the men being free of duty, they could not go to the nearby entertainment metropolis of Grantham. According to a rule that had been issued from the authorities, they had no access to the town more than once every seven to eleven days. In the squadron diary, it was noted, "As far as we know, the 61st Group is the only group of the entire Troop Carrier Command that has been placed under such restrictions. The men were cursing over life in Europe being so tedious." The airmen must have been cursing Denis

Kendall, the right-wing extremist MP, who was working so diligently at keeping them out of town.

However, on Fourth of July, there was a new invitation organized to the young women of the town, and during the dance that evening at the Red Cross Club at the airbase, there were "more girls present than usual", as the diary put it, which was "most important to the morale factor." Earlier that day, Moh took Daisy up for a new personnel transport to a "secret destination" with three landings.[116] What these flights to a "secret destination" were all about, can be gleaned from the monthly summary for July, 1944 in the Squadron diary, "Overseas flying time was fattened this month of July as Fourteenth airplanes did their heaviest flying since the winter days of Sicily. The ships were kept busy shuttling back and forth from France, hauling freights of weapons, ammunitions, spare parts, etc onto the continent, and sometimes evacuating walking and litter patients to the United Kingdom. Patients were also flown up to Prestwick, the Air Transport Command base in Scotland, for air transportation to the United States."

On July 6, Moh practiced towing gliders in formation with Daisy, and the next day, there were three practice landings for two and a half hours.[117] This was on a Friday, and from the WAAF* at the RAF Hospital in South Rauceby six miles northeast of Barkston Heath came a very pleasant invitation for a dance night that evening to celebrate the WAAF's fifth anniversary.[118]

On July 8, Daisy and eight other aircraft from the squadron flew a total of 173 wounded soldiers, who had been retrieved in France, to Prestwick. That evening, the dance night from the previous day with the WAAF was repeated. "The officers had a dance this evening with the usual good time," it was noted in the unit dairy.

On July 10, Daisy and three other aircraft from the squadron performed a true "flight show" for the people of Grantham by flying

---

* WAAF, *Women's Auxiliary Air Force,* was formed in 1939, reaching a membership of 180,000 during the war.

On July 6, 1944 Moh practiced towing gliders in formation with Daisy. (Norbert Moh's photo album. Via Cheryl Moh Grau.)

back and forth across town with double gliders behind each aircraft, something that nobody in town had ever seen before.[119]

After that, Daisy carried out an ordinary practice flight. The next day, Moh took her to a new "secret destination" which at the same tie was a navigation exercise. On July 12, he was in control of her during an exercise where they were dropping British paratroopers over Ropsley Heath east of Grantham. Two days later, there was a formation flight exercise, and on July 17, Daisy was flown to Wittering and back in formation with gliders in tow. The next day, Moh and Martzen took turns flying her on a new mission to a "secret destination" with three landings. They returned to Barkston Heath after three hours and twenty minutes. After having practiced towing gliders in formation to Wittering and back on the 19th, Moh flew new wounded soldiers who had been retrieved in France to Prestwick on the 20th, a flight that took five hours.[120]

On July 21, Barkston Heath had a grandiose visit by the Mexican revolutionary hero and aviation pioneer, General Gustavo Salinas Caminas. The general arrived in a Consolidated C-87 Liberator Express* from the air transport command.[121] The men at Barkston

---
* The civilian version of the four-engine bomber B-24 Liberator.

Heath stood wide-eyed at the imposing Mexican, who was a legend all over the Western Hemisphere. During the Mexican revolution in 1914, he had been the first one in the New World to drop bombs from an aircraft. He was now the commander of the Mexican Air Force. In honor of the general, a large formation flight was arranged, in which Daisy took part as well. That evening, the unit's orchestra, which had named itself The Skymasters, played at the Red Cross Aviation Club.[122]

The squadron's diary notes for July 24 read: "Of the 14th TCS's 20 aircraft, 18 were kept busy flying freight and personnel all over England, to say nothing of the flights to the continent. The only 2 ships that didn't get the call to come to work were No. 42-xx099, on DS, and the old standby No. 42-32913, which was out for some reason or other. At 0620 Lt. Colonel Lewis S. Frederich and Captain Willard C. Boyer addressed the EM's reveille formation on some rather vital subjects: venereal disease and so forth." Moh flew Daisy to "secret destinations" for seven hours and forty minutes, including six landings. On July 26, there was a formation exercise and four landings. Two days later, Moh first flew Daisy to Base 466, and after that, with cargo to a "secret destination" in France, before returning to Barkston Heath.[123]

Around this time, all documents were completed in a matter that the squadron had been spending quite a lot of time and work on, to adopt two orphan English children. These arrived on July 29. In the Squadron diary, we read, "Two very blonde English youngsters by the names of Ronald W. and Eileen W. [brother and sister] arrived in camp this evening accompanied by a comely American Red Cross girl." The next day, it was noted in the same diary, "Ronald W. and Eileen W., eight and ten years old, respectively, had a day they'll probably never forget. They were feted at a special dinner; they were special guests on a neighboring farm; they posed for photographers, including Lawrence O'Reilly of American Pathe News; they had the run of the base; Ronald was made an honorary Captain in the Air Forces and claims the distinction of being the only soldier on the base to monkey with the Colonel's shoulder Eagles and still stand in good stead." The same day, Moh carried out a personnel transport for four hours and forty minutes with Daisy to Exeter and back.

Training activities continued. Daisy flew in formation on August 3 and 5, and on the 7th, Moh took her up to drop paratroopers by night. On August 8, there were more training jumps from Daisy. Moh landed three times to pick up new paratroopers. In total, Daisy was airborne for four hours and five minutes that day. On August 10, Moh and Martzen took Daisy up in the air three times.[124] The same evening, the entire unit was ordered to Leicester, some twenty miles southwest of Grantham, where General Dwight D. Eisenhower, the Allied Supreme Commander in Europe, was going to address them. Eisenhower held a speech before a large assembly of paratroopers and transport aviation personnel. He told them that a new airborne unit, the First Allied Airborne Army, was being formed, and that it would consist of both paratrooper units and transport aviation units. When he mentioned "future operations," many groaned. But Eisenhower just grinned. He said that he knew they all wanted to go home—so did he; he loved fishing. But if you want to go home now, he continued, you do not belong in the airborne forces. Everybody was wondering what he meant by future operations. "Don't tell us we're going to train as an airborne army for operations in the East," somebody in the audience remarked. The men of the 61st TCG returned to Barkston Heath full of speculation.[125]

Exercise pace was now intensified. On August 11, Moh practiced landing with troops in Saltby with Daisy, and the next day, he took her up no less than six times, with a total flight time of four hours and forty-five minutes. After that, the 61st Group was deployed for a few days' transport flights to Normandy. Between August 13 and 16, Daisy flew once a day to Normandy and back, amongst other things with three-inch artillery shells on the way out and wounded soldiers on the way back.[126] Meanwhile, the squadron was supplied with a number of pilots and crews from the air transport command, as well as three aircraft, whereby the squadron's aircraft roster increased to twenty-six. This, and Eisenhower's speech, definitely ended any rumors that the unit would be dissolved. Instead, the men asked themselves when they would be sent into battle the next time, and where. Nobody knew yet—not even Eisenhower.

A few days of pouring rain gave the airmen a little rest. They took advantage of this by going to Stratford-upon-Avon on August 19, the birthplace of Shakespeare, where they saw Macbeth being performed at the Shakespeare Memorial Theatre. Afterwards, they made the happy discovery that the local pub, The Dirty Duck, was not only well-stocked with all kinds of alcoholic beverages, but that it also was a watering hole for the female actors from Shakespeare Memorial Theatre.[127] (The Dirty Duck, just next to the theater, remains to this day.)

On August 23 and 24, Daisy flew wounded that had been picked up in Normandy by other aircraft to Prestwick once each day. On August 25, twenty of the squadron's aircraft, one of them being Daisy, flew fuel that had first been picked up at Base 466 to Normandy. Moh logged six hours and fifty minutes in the air, the last thirty minutes of which were in darkness.[128] None of these flights to Normandy in August, 1944 cost the squadron any losses.

At fourteen minutes past midnight on August 28, the entire unit, including Daisy, took off to let newly trained paratroopers carry out their first nighttime jump. The airmen returned after two hours and got into bed at three o'clock in the morning.[129]

The build-up of the unit's force betrayed the fact that something big was underway. On August 31, Daisy and several other C-47s were used for fetching new gliders to Barkston Heath, so that the squadron now had 42 at its disposal. In addition, several new glider crews arrived.[130]

Something big really was underway. Ever since the airborne divisions had returned to England from Normandy in July, 1944, the Allied commanders were impatient to send them in again—such a large force as 30,000 elite soldiers could not be kept inactive. The operation that Eisenhower had in mind at the rally at Leicester on

Moh and Daisy during a training in towing gliders in formation. (Norbert Moh's photo album. Via Cheryl Moh Grau.)

August 10, 1944, was Operation "Transfigure," which had been planned in July, 1944. According to this, the airborne units were to be landed behind the German units that held the Allied pinned down at the bridgehead in Normandy. It was for this purpose that the First Allied Airborne Army was formed. On August 13, the countdown for this operation began, as the airborne units were being made ready. But at the same time, the situation on the ground in Normandy changed. The ground units achieved the much-coveted breakthrough by themselves, and having taken Dreux, west of Paris—the intended landing area for the airborne units—Operation "Transfigure" was called off on August 17.

However, at the same time as "Transfigure," another plan was being developed, under the code name "Boxer." The idea was to land the units at Boulogne at the Pas de Calais in order to take the areas from which the Germans had been firing their V1 flying bombs since June, 1944. This, however, soon turned out to be superfluous, as the British Air Defence became so efficient by August that it shot down as much as 90 percent of all incoming V1s. The V1 was, after all, only a pilotless aircraft flying at 400 mph, that is, not even as fast as the most modern British fighters.

Two other operations involving airborne units were also planned, "Linnet" I and II, and "Axehead," in order to cut off the German units' line of retreat from Normandy, but they all had to be cancelled because of the total collapse of the German units in France and the subsequent Allied lightning advance. This advance was begun at River Seine on August 29, 1944, and moved forward at breakneck speed, without envountering more than weak and uncoordinated resistance. On September 2, the British crossed the Franco-Belgian border, the next day, Brussels was liberated, and on September 4, the port city of Antwerp was taken.

The collapse of the German armies on the Western front—which was also a collapse of their morale—gave Field Marshal Bernard Montgomery, commander of the British-Canadian units in the West, the idea to use the paratroopers for a combined ground and air assault so as to open the way for the ground units for a quick thrust into the Ruhr area in Germany by taking bridges in hostile territory. The first draft of such a plan was called "Comet" and aimed at gaining control of the bridges across the Rhine between Arnhem and Wesel in the border area between Germany and central Netherlands, keeping these until the British Second Army cold reach them.

After the air force had advised Montgomery against deploying airborne forces against Wesel because of the very strong German flak at the Ruhr area, he modified "Comet" so that the operation was aimed at Arnhem, where there was a very important road bridge across the Rhine. By moving the previously planned advance by the Second Army to the west, and setting the eastern shore of the Zuiderzee as the first goal, the German units in western Netherlands would be isolated at the first stage. The objective, Montgomery, explained, was to "wipe out the enemy west of the Zwolle-Deventer-Kleve-Venlo-Maastricht line, with the purpose of then attacking west and occupying the Ruhr area."

Moh during an exercise in taking off in formation, probably with Daisy. (Norbert Moh's photo album. Via Cheryl Moh Grau.)

The First Canadian Army was to be concentrated across a twenty-mile sector in northern Belgium, aimed at the Netherlands. Via Eindhoven and Nijmegen, the advance would first take place towards Arnhem, a distance by road of seventy-five miles, and, from there, further towards Emmeloord, on the eastern side of the Zuiderzee, and then setting up bridgeheads on the eastern side of River IJssel, the Rhine tributary that runs northwards just east of Arnhem. By acting quickly and exploiting the fact that the Germans had moved forward most of their new units to northern Belgium, where Montgomery expected them to be crushed, the plan predicted a lightning advance over six days. After that, it was time for the next phase of the operation, a push towards the German Ruhr area.

Just as in "Comet," the ground assault would be combined with an airborne operation, the purpose of which being to secure important crossings over bodies of water along the planned assault route. The force of the airborne units that were to be deployed was increased from one and one brigade to three divisions and one brigade. These would, in Montgomery's words, lay "a carpet" for the British ground forces across eight bodies of water:

From south to north:
1. The Wilhelmina Canal north of Eindhoven.
2. The river Dommel in Sint-Oedenrode, four miles further north.

3. The Zuid-Willemsvaart Canal, another three miles north.
4. The parallel river Aa, one mile further north.
5. The bridge across the Maas at Grave, twenty miles to the northeast.
6. At least one of the bridges across the Maas-Waal Canal, yet another six miles away.
7. At least one of the bridges across the river Waal at Nijmegen, six miles further north.
8. At least one of the Rhine bridges on the southern outskirts of Arnhem, yet another ten miles to the north.

Montgomery delegated the fine-tuning of the details to his generals. It fell on the headquarters of the airborne army to hammer out the landing itself. Therefore, the operation eventually consisted of two assault plans: Operation "Market," the airborne part, and Operation "Garden," the ground operation—put together, "Market Garden." The U.S. 101st Airborne Division was entrusted with the objectives 1-4 above, the U.S. 82nd Airborne Division with objectives 5-7, and the British 1st Airborne Division with objective 8.

The Allies had upwards of 1,700 operational transport aircraft at their disposal—1,274 American and 164 British Douglas C-47s and 321 four-engine RAF bombers that could be deployed to tow gliders. In addition, there were more than 3,000 gliders, almost 2,200 Wacos, more than 900 Horsas, and 64 of the giant Hamilcars. The gliders being used by the American troop carrier units were Waco CG-4s, which could take either 13 soldiers or four passengers and one jeep, or three passengers and one 75mm howitzer.

In theory, this armada could fly in the 33,791 men from the three airborne divisions and the brigade that were earmarked for the assault in one single flight. But, with all the equipment that these units brought along, the number was limited to 16,500 men at any one time. Moreover, the Major General Paul L. Williams, commander of U.S. IX Troop Carrier Command, thought that there would not be enough time to service the aircraft and get another airborne operation going during one single day with the necessary concentration, as the flight units were based in England, as much as 400 miles by air from the landing zones (taking into consideration that the route had been calculated to avoid German flak as much as possible). With the C-47's cruising speed, it meant that the aircraft were airborne for more than six hours, including the time it took to assemble the formations. According to Williams, it was complicated enough to organize such a giant air operation in one day.

Neither did they want to fly in by night, which probably was a wise decision. The previous military Allied landings—in North

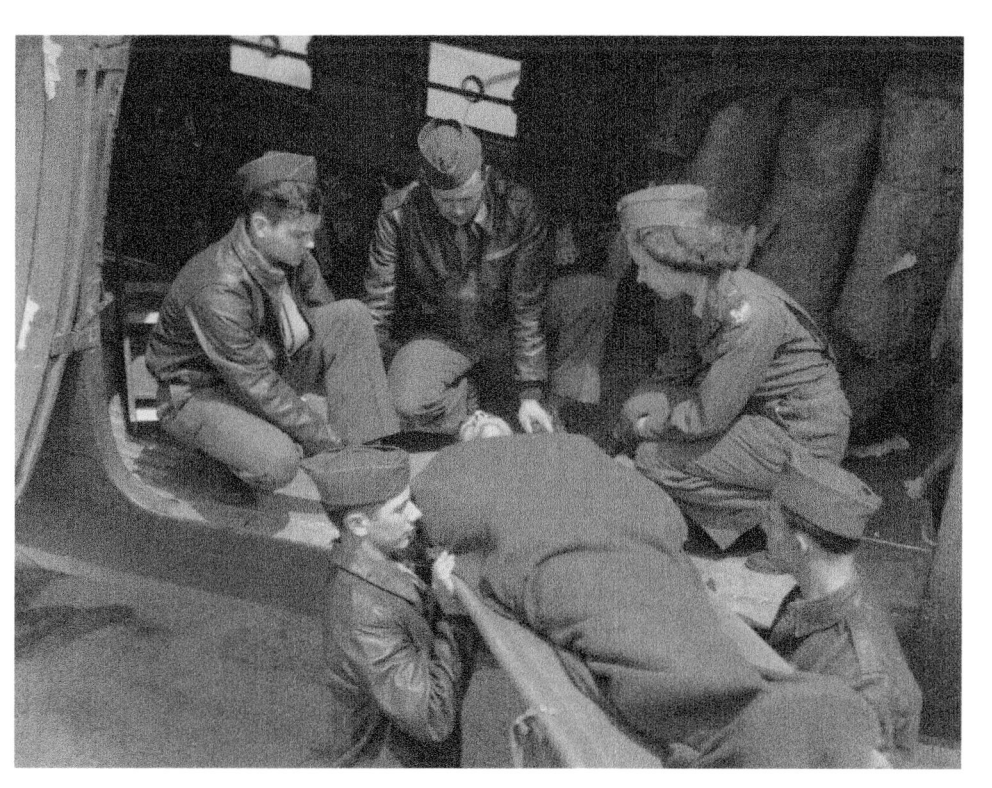

Wounded American soldiers are being evacuated from France in order to be flown to Prestwick for further transport to the U.S. (Photo: Norbert Moh. Via Cheryl Moh Grau.)

Africa, Italy, and Normandy—had all taken place during moonlit nights. But when "Market Garden" was begun, the moon was down, which made it very difficult to drop the paratroopers over the right spot. Moreover, the German night fighters had been weak in these other areas, but over Holland, very strong German night fighter units were operating. The German day fighters, on the other hand, was heavily decimated, and did not constitute an equally large threat, why it became natural to plan the landings for daytime. One thing that extended the time before the entire intended airborne force had been landed even further was the need to fly in supplies to the forces that had been landed first. Therefore, the plan for Operation "Market" would eventually comprise air landings for three consecutive days. It was all to be launched on September 17. Again, they would be using pathfinders with "Eureka" radios to aid the air crews to find the right drop zones.

Ahead of "Market Garden," the Allied transport aviation was deployed to deliver supplies to the British ground units in Belgium. On September 11 and 13, Moh flew such a mission each of the two days. On the last day, ammunition was delivered to Base B-58, the advance British airbase at Brussels. Meanwhile, on September 12, there was a personnel transport to the British Kemble airbase. After this, Daisy for some reason remained on the ground for three days, while Moh carried out two flights with other aircraft, one of which were to deliver supplies to Belgium.[131] It is possible that the September 13 mission was the flight that Moh later recounted, "During one flight when I had been delivering ammunition, one of the engines on my airplane cut out over the sea on the way back."[132] This could explain why Daisy remained on the ground while other aircraft were busy transporting supplies to the frontline units.[133]

On Saturday, September 16, everybody realized that the time had come, when a large number of British paratroopers arrived by truck at Barkston Heath. These were the so-called "Red Devils," tough elite soldiers who carried their maroon berets with pride. They were

Yanks Adopt Two Orphans

FÊTED IN STYLE AND GIVEN THE FREEDOM OF THE AIRFIELD!

Two London orphans had the time of their lives recently, when they were given the freedom of an American airfield in our district during the weekend.

The children, Eileen and Ronald, aged 10 and 8, are brother and sister. Their mother and father being dead, they have been adopted by a squadron of the U.S. Air Force, and now live with their grandparents.

On the Saturday they were brought from town by the Red Cross for their first visit to the country, and their kindly hosts took them to a nearby farmhouse for fresh eggs, milk and butter. Appreciating to the full their new experience, the children were thrilled to see farm animals.

On the Sunday, at the station where they had stayed the night, they were given a big dinner, followed by handfuls of gum, candy and oranges, and they had their photographs taken in the planes by Corporal Harry Portman of Boston, Massachusetts, official photographer at the base. Larry O'Reilly, war correspondent for Pathe News Inc., took a series of movie shots of the children. The enlisted men gave them a great welcome, and had a special cake made for them.

Given command of the field, the children just expressed a wish, and it was carried out. Jeeps were painted with their names, and they were allowed to steer; a formation of 'planes flew specially overhead, and when the 'planes were grounded, Ronald and Eileen used the radio to call in to the station. The crowning glory for Ronald, however, was when he was made an honorary captain of the Ninth Air Force.

The photograph above shows part of the reception committee which greeted the new members at the station and accompanied them to the base. Ronnie's first gift was a new hat, and, as can be seen, he paid little attention to its fit. He later returned it as it would not conform with regulations and his newly acquired promotion to an honorary captain.

Pictured from left to right are: Major Lewis S. Frederick, jun., commanding officer of the squadron, Shelbyville, Kentucky; Technical - Sergeant Albert J. Mazalesky, Nanticoke, Pennsylvania, Eileen; Firs.- Sergeant Clair A. Cole, Rochester, Pennsylvania; Miss Patricia Ellis, American Red Cross, Great Britain; 1st-Lieutenant Berlin A. Roberts, Greenfield, Indiana; Ronald; Miss Juanita Pagella, American Red Cross, Palo Alto, California; 2nd-Lieutenant Albertto F. Perna, Waltham, Massachusetts; Pfc Stanley B. Golec, Detroit, Michigan; and Cpl. Raymond R. Yokel, Pittsburgh, Pennsylvania.

Friday, August 11, 1944, the local newspaper Grantham Journal published an article about the two orphans Eileen and Ronald that the men of the 14th Troop Carrier Squadron had decided to adopt. (Via John Burgess, Grantham Journal.)

Squatting left in the image in *Grantham Journal*, Major Lewis J. Frederick, commander of the 14th Troop Carrier Squadron, can be seen. Between the two female American Red Cross members Patricia Ellis (left) and Juanita Pagella (right) are the two children Eileen and Ronald.

to constitute the spearhead of the operation that was intended to finish the war before Christmas; they were the ones who were to be dropped at Arnhem.

Sunday, September 17, dawned with bright sunshine. At around eight o'clock in the morning, ground fog descended on the fields, but it soon lifted. The air crews were summoned to the briefing room, where the June 5 procedure was basically repeated. Colonel Mitchell, the intelligence commander, Captain Augustine Stoney, and the meteorologist, Captain Benjamin Piacentini each addressed the men to prepare then. The Army Chaplain Captain Kenneth Combs said a prayer for the airmen, and after that, the men left the room, each one with their own thoughts.

Meanwhile, more British paratroopers had arrived. One of them, Norman Hicks, recounts, "We left Donington by truck for the short journey to RAF Barkston Heath [60 kilometers east] on the morning of Sunday 17th September 1944. It was a lovely, clear day on what was to be my third operation. Arriving early, we gathered in small groups and after all the activity were able to laze on the grass – we even had time for a cup of tea before kitting up in preparation for our aircraft number being called."[134] Brigadier Gerald William Lathbury, commander of the 1st Parachute Brigade of the British 1st Airborne Division, wrote in his diary, "Sunday, September 17th dawned a lovely day except for ground haze. Got to Barkston Heath Airfield at about 1015 a.m. Everyone in fine spirits."[135]

In all, there were almost 900 men—from the 1st Parachute Brigade, the 1st Company of the Airborne Artillery, and the 1st Airborne Division's headquarters—waiting to board the khaki painted C 47s of the 61st Troop Carrier Group. The paratroopers also received clerical blessings, as Hicks recalled, "As had become our custom, the padre took us to one side and held a short Roman Catholic service in the shadow of the aircraft. With the padre's blessing, we lined up to board. This was no easy matter as we were carrying so much kit that we had to be helped up the steps of the aircraft by the US ground crew. "Eventually, with much shuffling and bumping, we settled in, ably assisted by the crew chief [in Daisy's case, Sergeant William Gray was crew chief] who offered help as our kit snagged everything we passed. We were now ready, we were kitted and loaded. Below the aircraft our containers were secured in the racks where they had been hung the previous day."[136]

Another one of the paratroopers, Herbert Butcher, said, We were tied up tighter than Christmas parcels for overseas mailing, over our battledresses and airborne smocks was our equipment, ammunition pouches, waterbottles, entrenching tools, messtins, etc. etc. all held together with belts and braces, plus whatever other odds and end we needed for our own particular job, in my case a havesack of batteries. Then came the jumping jackets, a loose denim affair, zipped down the front, to stop everything else flopping about and getting tangled in the parachute. Then came the lifejacket, just incase we came down in the sea. Next came the parachute and finally the Sten gun and magazines tucked into the harness. We must have all at last resembled that favourite epithet of sergeant-majors, pregnant nuns."[137]

A less-known fact is that some of the British airborne soldiers carried protective vests, as described by Butcher, "Another item available to key personnel was body armour. It consisted of a padded steel plate that hung over the chest with another, about half its size hung from the webbing straps to protect the stomach and a tee-shaped back piece to shield the kidneys." Brigadier Lathbury noted in his diary: "Emplaned 1115 a.m." [138]

In each of the 14th TCS's eighteen aircraft, seventeen paratroopers took their seats. The Squadron's mission was to transport 306 of the 548 men in Lieutenant Colonel David Dobie's* 1st Battalion of the 1st Parachute Brigade.

Several units with a large number of aircraft were passing by in the air above while the fully loaded C-47s were rolling out onto the runway. At the front was Colonel Mitchell's aircraft. After him, the entire 14th TCS followed, before the other squadrons. At 1121 hours, the aircraft started rolling out onto the runway and take to the skies. At 1152 hours, all of the squadron's aircraft were airborne, and joined the other squadrons of the wing. At 1214 hours, the formation set off.[139]

From a vast number of other airports—Saltby, Fulbeck, Balderton, Langar, Folkingham, and may others—hundreds of transport aircraft came buzzing. They flew low, at only fifteen hundred feet, and the mighty rumble from hundreds of Twin Wasp engines made people pour out of their houses all the way from Barkston Heath to Aldeburgh, forty miles east of Cambridge, where they flew out over the North Sea. The War Diary of the 52nd Troop Carrier Wing noted that all of its aircraft took off without any problems, and that not one of them had to abort because of any technical faults.

By now, the weather was almost completely clear. Below, the many shadows from the aircraft, moving forward like a great cloud,

---

* Both Lathbury and Dobie were captured at Arnhem but managed to escape and were hidden by the Dutch Resistance until they made it across the Rhine in October 1944, to the Allied lines.

Barkston Heath in the morning of September 17, 1944: Men from the 1st Battalion of British 1st Parachute Brigade are waiting to be flown to Arnhem. The aircraft in the background could very well be Daisy. Standing second from the left is Albert Osborne, who was killed on September 21, 1944. Bottom far right is the Canadian 2nd Lieutenant Leo Heaps, who wrote two books after the war about the Battle of Arnhem, *Escape* and *The Grey Goose of Arnhem*. (Signal Corps, Murray T. Poznak.)

could be seen on an almost completely calm sea. Throughout the flight across the water, which took 40 minutes, there were sea rescue boats beneath them, ready to act if any aircraft would be forced to make an emergency landing. "Very good flight, but a bit chilly. "Lovely and calm over the sea," Lathbury commented.[140] Sergeant Bruce Cox, one of the British paratroopers, describes the approach, "I looked out the window again, this was a sight I never wanted to forget. Down through the formation came four '109s, followed by about 20 Spitfires. Not a shot was fired at our planes. We could see the coastline now; not too much longer to go."[141]

Then, the armada swept in over the Dutch coast, at the lighthouse on the island of Schouwen. This had been given the code name "Bermuda" on the flight maps.[142]

In Crailo, near Amsterdam, the German military commander for the Netherlands, *General* Friedrich Christiansen, was having dinner together with his Chief of Staff, *Generalleutnant* Heinz-Hellmuth von Wühlisch, when they suddenly heard an almighty roar of engines from the south. The immediately got in touch with the command post, which reported that many hundreds of transport aircraft had flown in across the Scheldt Estuary heading east, probably towards Arnhem. Von Wühlisch advised against sanding any troops there; he believed that Arnhem was "lost," but Christiansen objected that he was much too afraid of Hitler, who would hardly appreciate such a defeatist approach.[143] The two terrified men asked themselves what to do, and agreed to call Field Marshal Walter Model, commander of Army Group "B."

Model had his command post located at Hotel Tafelberg in the little town of Oosterbeek, west of Arnhem. There, they responded

Daisy and the other C-47s of the 14th Troop Carried Squadron ahead of takeoff from Barkston Heath on September 17,1944. (Signal Corps, Murray T. Poznak.)

that the Field Marshal was having lunch at Hotel Hartenstein, where the mess was located, but they were put through to *Generalleutnant* Hans Krebs, Model's Chief of Staff. Krebs was very nervous—von Wühlich had the impression that he was barely listening to what he had to say—and just said, "We're leaving immediately!"[144]

Initially, Daisy and the other aircraft mostly flew across flooded land, but soon, the men saw houses and villages, and soon, Dutchmen came pouring out of these, leaping and waving enthusiastically with both arms at the passing aircraft. These continued due east to a point south of the town 's-Hertogenbosch, at Vught, where the entire armada turned left. It was in Vught that *Generaloberst* Kurt Student, who led the German paratroop units, happened to have his command post. He was given a right ringside seat for this grandiose air show, which he could not help being impressed by. Student recounted:

> "It was a beautiful late summer day. My H.Q. was, since a few days, at Vught (south of s'-Hertogenbosch), in a cottage. There was general quietness along the front line. Before noon, the enemy activity in the air suddenly became very great. I noticed from my house numerous formations of fighter-bombers and heard bombs falling, firing from aircraft guns and AA. artillery. About noon I was disturbed at my desk by a roaring in the air which more and more increased in intensity so that I left my study and went onto the balcony. Wherever I looked I saw aircraft: troop-transport airplanes and large airplanes towing gliders. They flew in formation and they flew singly. It was an immense stream which passed at quite a low height near the house. I was greatly impressed by this mighty spectacle. I must confess that during these minutes I did not think of the danger of the situation but reflected with regret the memory of my own airborne operations, and when my Chief of Staff* entered, I could not say more to him but: 'Oh, how I wish I had ever such powerful means at my disposal!'"[145]

The aircraft armada transporting the British paratroopers only met weak resistance from German flak—a good testimonial to the preparatory airstrikes and the fighter escort—and not one of the transport aircraft was shot down.

Meanwhile, there was a call from Hotel Tafelberg to Hotel Hartenstein in Oosterbeek, announcing that there was something urgent. Model's First General Staff Officer, Colonel Hans-Georg von Tempelhoff, calmly rose from the dinner table and went to the telephone room. His calm was soon swept away by what he heard. He had barely hung up after being given the ominous message before a series of powerful exploding bombs blew out the windows, sending shards of glass flying around the room. Everybody threw themselves for cover under the table, and then ran out into the yard. At that very moment, the transport air armada appeared. The sky seemed completely black with aircraft. Von Tempelhoff came running down the stone stairs, yelling to drown out the rumble from the aircraft's engines, "What a great big mess! One or two divisions of paratroopers are over us!" Model quickly made his decision, "Everybody out!" he ordered, leaping into the staff car, which quickly drove away.[146]

The paratroopers were to have begun jumping at 1340 hours, but the foremost formation, the 314th TCG, came in ten minutes late. The 61st TCG, which followed suit, managed better. It regained much of its lost time and came in at 1408 hours, only six minutes after the designated time.[147]

Daisy and all the other transport aircraft roared ahead above the roofs of the houses in the small town of Renkum. Ahead of them, large fields spread out, littered with gliders and swarming with soldiers in vivacious activity. These belonged to the 1st Glider Brigade, which had been landed at around one o'clock. White marking strips, blue smoke, and "Eureka" transmitters confirmed that this was Landing Zone "X," which was the target. Among the houses in Oosterbeek and Arnhem to the east, and from the town of Ede somewhat north, fires and black clouds of smoke could be seen, the results of the preparatory Allied bomb raids.[148]

The paratroopers were ready, with all their muscles tense. William Gray and all crew chiefs aboard the aircraft had alerted them when there were twenty minutes left to the estimated time of arrival. The soldiers checked their harnesses one last time, and then stood up and formed a line ending at the jump hatch on the left side of the aircraft. This had, as was customary, remained open throughout the flight. The first men in line could look out over the landscape moving by just below them. The men felt the overhead guide wire that would deploy their parachutes automatically, through a wire that was connected to it. Five minutes ahead of the estimated time of arrival, the red "jump light" went on. It was the crew navigator who had to estimate when he would switch on the green light, which was the signal to jump.

Norbert Moh reduced the throttle as much as he could to just above the C-47's stall speed, around 90 knots, and carefully pushed the stick forward so that the aircraft went into a slight dive—this was to raise the tail so that the paratroopers would not risk bumping into it when jumping.

Sergeant Bruce Cox recounts, "Then all of a sudden, 'Stand up. Hook up. Check lines and equipment.' My legs were wobbling, must be all this bloody weight; full G.1098 fighting gear. Looking outside I could see green fields. The engine's revs died down. 'Stand to the door.' Red was on. 'Green on. GO.' Static line straps were banging. Move it, boys, move it!"[149]

Sped up by William Gray, the seventeen paratroopers disappeared out of the hatch in quick succession. Eventually, only the guide wire was left, which Gray pulled in. Meanwhile, Moh turned Daisy away while climbing to the left.

"Suddenly I am gone," Bruce Cox remembers, "and automatically start checking my gear and looking for smoke—that's the place I have to head towards. I can hear the crack of small arms. The ground is coming up, I assume landing position and remember to roll, keeping low. Another guy lands nearby; he looks scared, but gives the thumbs up and we both start moving. A cannister crashes to the ground—

chute didn't deploy. Let's get out of this DZ, it could be dangerous!" Private Stephen George Morgan recounts, "Weighing me down were not only my Lee Enfield No. 4 rifle but my ration packs, 2 Hawkins anti-tank mines and three sealed boxes containing 250 rounds each for our Vickers machine gun. After landing I released my parachute and emptied my kitbag of three boxes of machine gun ammunition

Aboard an aircraft from the 14th Troop Carrier Squadron on its way to Arnhem on September 17, 1944. Left row from the front: Sergeant P. Kelly (later captured in Arnhem), Private Hellier, Corporal James Court, Private John Fairweather (KIA on September 18, 1944), Lance Corporal Lawrence Brown (KIA on September 25, 1944), unknown, Private John Cortman (KIA on September 18, 1944), Private Ron Tidbal, unknown. Right row from the front: Private Gibbons, Corporal Mount, Private Henry McAnelly, Sergeant Jack Reynolds, four unidentified. The image is taken from the back, and the cockpit is visible through the open cabin door. (Signal Corps, Murray T. Poznak.)

and two Hawkins anti-tank mines. A German reconnaissance vehicle appeared with a small armored car and an open topped lorry full of soldiers. As I was about a hundred yards behind, I was not part of the fight but saw all the German soldiers either killed or captured."[150]

As the transport aircraft flew back towards England, the Germans were better prepared, and met the aircraft with more intense flak. "During the return flight, the German flak forced us to fly at absolutely maximum speed at treetop altitude," Moh recounted, continuing, "And still, another plane overtook me."[151] But all aircraft made it. At 1600 hours, they began returning to Barkston Heath, and at 1640 hours, the last aircraft had landed.[152] One single paratrooper returned, since he had been unable to jump due to sickness. The air operation was a complete success. The resistance they had met—limited to fire from the ground—had been inefficient. The only damage any of the aircraft of the 14th TCS had been caused was one small bullet hole in one machine (not Daisy) which did not do any damage worth mentioning.[153]

In spite of Daisy being undamaged, she did not participate in the following day's mission, when the unit dropped gliders with parts of the American 82nd Airborne Division south of Nijmegen. Moh participated with another aircraft. Several of the machines of the 14th Squadron were damaged by flak and one was shot down.[154]

The next mission in connection with Operation "Market" was planned for September 19. On that day, the Polish Parachute Brigade was to be dropped south of the road bridge in Arnhem, but because of dens ground fog, the flight had to be cancelled. There, the bad luck with the weather that hit "Market Garden" began. The bad weather continued for four days, which meant that the British paratroopers lost their stronghold on the northern side of the road bridge in Arnhem, which they had taken on the first day. It was not until September 23 that the transport aircraft at the northern airbases in England could be deployed again. By then, the mission was to fly in the 325th Glider Regiment of 82nd U.S. Airborne Division to the so-called "Drop Zone Oscar" in the fields just north of River Maas at the Dutch town of Grave, some twelve miles southwest of Arnhem as the crow flies.

Twenty-one C-47s, one of them being Daisy with Moh in control, were hooked up to as many Waco gliders with American airborne soldiers.[155] Takeoff was planned to 1020 hours, but was postponed, at first to 1120 hours, then to 1220, and eventually to 1250, when the weather had cleared enough for the aircraft to be able to take off. They were part of the total of 408 C-47 Skytrains with as many Waco

A page in the war diary of the 14th Troop Carrier Squadron showing which ones of the unit's aircraft that participated in the landing of the British 1st Airborne Division at Arnhem on September 17, 1944. "732" means 43-30732, that is, Daisy.

gliders that brought about three thousand men from the Glider Regiment as well as 24 artillery pieces.

During the approach across the North Sea, the aircraft were disrupted by a heavy propwash from a large number of British four-engine aircraft flying right above them. These Short Stirlings were being used to fly in supplies that would be dropped to the British paratroopers who were still holding their own in Oosterbeek. Over the continent, the weather was mainly good, with visibility of up to five miles, even though the aircraft during part of the journey flew through some light rain. Flight altitude was 2,000 ft. The formation flight did not work as smoothly as on September 17—there was congestion in the air, forcing many pilots to slow down. Moh recounts, "The book indicates that air speeds towing gliders were 120 mph They were closer to 90 mph—about 70 mph to become airborne on takeoff."[156]

Drop Zone "Oscar" was held by the Allies, and in order to avoid flak, the entire approach was to be performed over areas controlled by friendlies. But the first few aircraft turned north too early, missing the wedge that the Allies held from Belgium and up to Nijmegen in the Netherlands. The entire approach was therefore carried out over hostile territory, and the aircraft were continuously fired on from the ground. In the beginning, this was quite weak, but ahead of them, the airmen could see huge clouds of smoke and explosions from a battle raging on the ground.

It was the Germans that had attacked the highway that constituted the only Allied line of supply during "Market Garden," dubbed "Club Route" (even though the American soldiers called it "Hell's Highway"). The battle was at its fiercest around the town of Veghel, some twelve miles ahead of Grave, when the transport aircraft came rumbling in. All the pilots were focusing on was Drop Zone "Oscar."

At that moment, the 33-year-old German *SS-Hauptsturmführer* Friedrich Richter was in the middle of the battle on the ground. He jumped up onto a tank and pointed towards the highway, "*Front zur Strasse, Feuer frei!*"—"Front towards the road, fire at will!" Then, he jumped down, and ran towards the canal a bit further away, passing two other tanks. *"Schiesst, Jungs, schiesst bis zur letzten Granate!"*—"Fire, guys, fire until the last grenade!"—he yelled at them. Then, he came across another SS officer, who reported that his assault guns were firing at the bridge across the canal in Veghel. Richter recounted: "I said, 'That's good! But keep a few shells as a reserve. The enemy is coming down the road with tanks, and if the Tommies break through, we're in a hole!' He replied, "Of course, *Hauptsturmführer!*' What a splendid man! It was sheer joy having a man like him with us. With new confidence, I ran back to my grenadier companies.

"But suddenly, I froze. To the left, the sky is blackening: At 200 to 300 meters' altitude, a terrific armada of transport aircraft with gliders in tow is coming. They're coming straight towards us, surrounded by bombers and fighter-bombers. The entire front has fallen silent. Not one shot is fired. Everything grinds to a halt. The fog has lifted and I'm looking upwards. It feels as though I'm alone in the whole world and an enormous beast is descending upon me.

Norbert Moh's pilot's logbook for September 1944.

I don't know for how long I remained like that, but I do know that my legs were trembling violently and that I couldn't make them stop. In groups of three, closely together, aircraft after aircraft is rumbling forward just overhead. They continue north and it never seems to end."[157]

Richter stood petrified until the commander of the Panzer Brigade 107 came up to him, shouting to drown out the roar of the engines, "Now what do we do?" Only then did Richter come to his senses. "Fire!" he cried. "Fire! Don't you have machine guns on your combat vehicles?"

Norbert Moh recounted*: "We ran into intense anti-aircraft fire. All four aircraft in our echelon were hit badly. The #2 aircraft was shot down. We sustained about a two-foot-in-diameter hole in our fuselage near the tail. Half of our elevator control cables were severed. We returned very gingerly, but safely."[158] After five hours and fifty minutes of flight, a completely exhausted Moh landed at Barkston Heath, where Daisy was immediately put aside for repairs.

This would become Moh's last flight with Daisy. On September 24, he did a test flight with the aircraft no. 42-32913, the one dubbed "the old reserve machine 913" in the war diary's notes.[159] Daisy made one very last flight with another pilot—unknown who—on September 29, when she was transporting personnel to a "secret destination."[160] After that, it seems as though her damages were considered making her too unreliable to fly. Throughout the rest of the war, Daisy by all accounts remained on the ground—there are no notes of any flights with her in the 14th Squadron's war diary, which had logged very single aircraft's flights right up until May, 1945.

At the beginning of October, Norbert Moh was transferred to the pathfinder school at Chalgrove near Oxford, where he was trained in

---

* According to Moh, this flight took place on September 21, but his pilot's logbook shows that he did not fly at all on that day. This is confirmed by the 14th Troop Carrier Squadron's War Diary, which notes for September 21, "No flying this date." The only day consistent with Moh's description above is September 23, 1944.

using the latest navigation aids in order to lead an entire formation towards a target. After that, he continued flying with the 14th TCS during the rest of October, November, and December, 1944.[161] He recounted, "During the Battle of the Bulge, we were waiting and waiting for the weather to clear so that we could fly in supplies and reinforcements. On Christmas Eve, we flew supplies into France. We landed in an open field and spent the night freezing inside our aircraft. On Christmas Day, we managed to return to the only airbase that was open in England, at Brighton. We had fresh eggs for Christmas dinner! After New Year's Day, I had gathered enough points to be able to return stateside."[162]

On January 2, 1945, Moh made his last flight with the 14th TCS, a harmless flight within the coasts of England. Two days later, it was time to go home. One of his comrades at the 14th TCS, 1st Lieutenant Albert Tissier, wrote, "Lt. Norbert D. Moh, an old-timer in the 14th, said good-bye to the outfit, and travelled the well-beaten path up to the 70th Replacement Depot at Stone."[163]

Moh recounted, "I flew from Prestwick to Washington with a C-54 via the Azores and Newfoundland. I was stationed at first at Ellington Airfield in Houston, and after that at Chanute in Champaign. Once, I made a trip to my home in Wisconsin, which drew all the kids out of their schools and made the farmers leave their tractors and the painters fall off their ladders. They'd never seen such a large airplane close up before. On my last flight, I fetched the famous baseball team from Chicago and flew them to Chanute. Bob Feller and Walker Cooper* were with me on that flight."[164]

For his military service, Moh was awarded the Air Medal with three Oak Leaves. After his discharge from the Army on September 28, 1954, he worked for 27 years as an air traffic controller, the last 20 years in Des Moines. After that, he worked for the Alpha Travel

---

* Bob Feller (1918-2010) and Walker Cooper (1915-1991) were two of the most famous American baseball players in those days.

Agency until retirement. He and his wife May had two children, Cheryl in 1946 and Shelley in 1950.

In 1975, Norbert Moh visited England together with his wife, and took the opportunity to go to Barkston Heath. He did not meet anyone he knew from the war but told *The Des Moines Tribune:* "Our old Quonset Huts remained at least, but now there are swine living I them, and in some they are growing mushrooms."[165]

On December 18, 1994, just after turning 75, Norbert Moh passed away.

Daisy flies on

World War II ended in Europe on May 8, 1945. On May 12 or 13, 1945, Daisy made a long flight to Trinidad, where she landed on May 16, 1945.[166] This was the 14th Troop Carrier Squadron's last base. On July 31, 1945, the unit was disbanded. Daisy remained in Trinidad until September 23, 1945, when she was flown to Morrison Airfield in Florida, where she, just as the other C-47s that had belonged to the 14th TCS, was registered as "superfluous." On October 24, 1945, Daisy was transferred to Bush Field, Georgia, where she was mothballed.[167] In 1946, she was bought by Canada Air Ltd, which rebuilt her into a civilian DC-3 by replacing the cargo hatch with a passenger door, fitting passenger seats, and soundproofing the fuselage. After that, she was sold to the Norwegian Airline Company Det Norske Luftselskap (DNL), which gave her the name "Nordfugl," the Northern Bird. By that time, the DNL's air fleet consisted of two Junkers 52s that the company had had since before the war, as well as another five Junkers 52s that had been taken over from the German Luftwaffe, two Douglas DC-4 Skymasters, and two old C-47s that had been rebuilt into DC-3s. Registered as LN-IAF, "Nordfugl" flew commercially to northern Norway and Europe.

On August 1, 1948, the DNL was merged with the Danish Airline Company Det Danske Luftselskab (DDL) and Sweden's AB Aerotransport into SAS. At the merger, all aircraft were painted in the SAS colors, and were branded with the company's emblems. The DC-3s and the DC-4s were all given names ending in Viking. In the case of our aircraft, it became "Fridtjof Viking."

In 1957, the aircraft was sold on to the Swedish Airline Company Linjeflyg, where she was re-registered as SE-CFP. Three years later, she was sold to the Swedish Air Force, which repainted her at the Bulltofta Airport, and again fitted the cargo doors and replaced the Twin Wasp engines with Swedish STWC-3-type copies. With the Air Force designation Tp 79 and again re-registered as 79006 (796), she

Daisy at the Västerås Airport in Sweden in July 2018. (Photo: The author.)

was first sent to Swedish Air Force Group F 7 *(Flygflottilj 7)* at Såtenäs Airfield, Sweden. In 1975, she was rented out to the Red Cross, which flew 325 tons of supplies and 826 people for organizations including Sweden's Save the Children during humanitarian efforts in Ethiopia. In 1978, she ended up at Swedish Air Force Group F 3 in Malmslätt, Sweden.

Daisy remained in the Swedish Air Force until 1982. Then, she was disposed of for SEK 70,000 to two civilians, Ingemar Wärme and Jimmie Berglund, who formed the Association of Flying Veterans (Föreningen Flygande Veteraner) the same year for the technical and financial management of the aircraft. In 1983, she was taken over by the newly-formed Flying Veterans' Foundation (Stiftelsen Flygande Veteraner). On June 20, 1984, the first members' flight was carried out with her, and six days later, she regained her old civilian registration SE-CFP, while being classed as a veteran aircraft.

So, what about the name Daisy? It came about through the Flying Veterans, and it was during a solemn ceremony at the Bromma Airport near Stockholm on October 4, 1985, that the aircraft was given this name. Interestingly enough, there is another name painted on her; for the 40th anniversary of the SAS in August, 1986, Daisy was repainted in SAS livery, and then, part of the ceremony was having "Fridtjof Viking" again painted onto her nose. However, her name is Daisy—even though she has actually appeared under yet another name: in 1990, Daisy made her movie debut, when she played an important part in the Swedish TV series "Tre Kärlekar" (Three Loves), then as "Örnen"/ SE-BAA in ABA:s old livery.

The same year, the Flying Veterans restored Daisy to her former condition in one important way, when they managed to get hold of two Pratt & Whitney R-1830 Twin Wasp engines, which were fitted instead of the STWC-3 copies.

Initially, Daisy was based at Bromma near Stockholm, but she has now been moved to Västerås Airport, sixty miles to the west, where she since 2013 has her winter abode. In 2018, she moved into the Västerås Aviation Museum. During the summers, there are regular members' flights with Daisy to various destinations. After the completed flying season in 2017, Daisy had a total of 34,069 hours and 34 minutes of flight time.

At the time of writing, Daisy is at Malmen in Linköping, where she is being repaired following an engine fire on July 13, 2018. However, Daisy will soon be in the air again, in spite of recently having turned 75.

The author in front of Daisy at the Västerås Airport in July, 2018. (Photo: The author.)

Appendix 1

Film Section

This is a Vaktel Multimedia Book. This means that the text is being supplemented not only by stills and maps, but also by video and audio clips. You can access these easily using your smartphone or tablet computer through so-called QR codes.

QR codes (Quick Response) are codes for optical scanning reminiscent of common bar codes. It is easy to download software that scans QR codes on your smartphone or tablet computer. After that, it is sufficient to hold your telephone with that software running above a QR code in order for the web page with the video clip in question to be opened.

There are many free QR scanner apps that you can download onto your smartphone or tablet computer. They can be downloaded from, for example, Apple's App Store or the Android Market, depending on which type of smartphone or tablet computer you are using.

Trailer for the movie D-Day: Down to Earth; on the 507th Parachute infantry Regiment.
https://www.youtube.com/watch?v=Pi3mW-Ytwk8

Paratroopers of the 82nd Airborne Division prepare for takeoff on June 5, 1944.
https://www.youtube.com/watch?v=a9434Oc2FM4

Color video: C-47s ahead of D-Day.
https://www.youtube.com/watch?v=idNbxUBof_U

Paratroopers of the 82nd Airborne Division board the aircraft in the evening of June 5, 1944, the aircraft take off, the approach.
https://www.youtube.com/watch?v=v2DA4wdiba8

Roy Creek, Commander of E Company of the 2nd Battalion of the 507th PIR recounts, footage from flying in the 82nd Airborne Division on June 6, 1944.
https://www.youtube.com/watch?v=PwEJbr8Hl2A

The sequence from "Band of Brothers" showing the parachute drop on D-Day.
https://www.youtube.com/watch?v=zCrw_uMWlgI

American wartime training film: How to Fly a C-47.
Part 1:
https://www.youtube.com/watch?v=e7sHZbLd8WE

Part 2:
https://www.youtube.com/ watch?v=vKyiHn7umWM&t=243s

Part 3:
https://www.youtube.com/watch?v=mln9T6OW3A4

The song "Rosie the Riveter" by Redd Evans and John Jacob Loeb with The Vagabonds.
https://www.youtube.com/watch?v=55NCElsbjeQ

The movie "The Lady Eve"—a sample.
https://www.youtube.com/watch?v=fZ7X5JDKmSI

The movie "Higher and Higher" starring Frank Sinatra and Michèle Morgan—a sample.
https://www.youtube.com/watch?v=RyEdD3izAw4

The veteran Stephen George Morgan remembers the airdrop at Arnhem on September 17, 1944.
https://www.youtube.com/watch?v=JU0za3parRE

00.00-05.33: Authentic wartime footage of the approach of the 1st Airborne Division and the landing at Arnhem on September 17, 1944.
https://www.youtube.com/watch?v=FXAyK8vDQhI

How to start a DC-3.
https://www.youtube.com/watch?v=bEYEcVQklvY

Air reconnaissance with DC-3 SE-CFP Daisy, May 9, 2015.
https://www.youtube.com/watch?v=BvZCFn1lo_8

Parachuting from DC-3 Daisy at Västerås.
https://www.youtube.com/watch?v=Fx-Obcnihvs

Gerald Parker, who flew a C-47 in the 61st Troop Carrier Group at the same time as Moh, flies a C-47 again in 2017. Parker passed away on October 18, 2017.
https://www.youtube.com/watch?v=5thY5l4G2kg

Appendix 2
Daisy's flights 1943-1945

Date	Mission	Takeoff	Landing	Pilot	Notes
17.10.43	Transit	Long Beach	Baer AAF Base	*	
Oct.-Nov. 1943	Trial flights *	Baer AAF Base		*	
12.11.43	Transit *		Marrakech, Marocko	*	
17.2.44	Transit	Marrakech	St. Mawgan, UK	Moh	
18.2.44	Transit	St. Mawgan, UK	Barkston Heath	Moh/Martzen	
3.3.44	Training	Barkston Heath	Barkston Heath	Moh/Martzen	
3.3.44	Training	Barkston Heath	Barkston Heath	Moh/Martzen	
4.3.44	Training	Barkston Heath	Barkston Heath	Moh	
4.3.44	Training	Barkston Heath	Barkston Heath	Moh	
5.3.44	Training	Barkston Heath	Barkston Heath	Moh	
7.3.44	Trial flight	Barkston Heath	Barkston Heath	Moh	
11.3.44	Training	Barkston Heath	Barkston Heath	Moh/Martzen	
16.3.44	Training	Barkston Heath	Barkston Heath	*	
19.3.44	Training	Barkston Heath	Barkston Heath	Moh/Martzen	
22.3.44	Training	Barkston Heath	Barkston Heath	Moh/Martzen	
22.3.44	Training	Barkston Heath	Barkston Heath	Martzen	Paratroop jump
23.3.44	Training	Barkston Heath	Barkston Heath	Moh/Martzen	
27.3.44	Training	Barkston Heath	Barkston Heath	Moh	Paratroop jump
28.3.44	Training	Barkston Heath	Barkston Heath	Moh/Martzen	Towing of gliders

Continued overleaf

Continued

Date	Mission	Takeoff	Landing	Pilot	Notes
29.3.44	Training	Barkston Heath	Barkston Heath	Moh	Flight time 15 mins.
5.4.44	Training	Barkston Heath	Barkston Heath	*	Paratroop jump
10.4.44	Transport	Barkston Heath	*	Moh	
10.4.44	*	*	Lanford Lodge	Moh	
10.4.44	Return	Lanford Lodge	Barkston Heath	Moh	
13.4.44	Training	Barkston Heath	Greenham Common	*	Transport of gliders
13.4.44	Training	Greenham Common	Barkston Heath	*	Transport of gliders
14.4.44	Training	Barkston Heath	Greenham Common	*	Transport of gliders
14.4.44	Training	Greenham Common	Barkston Heath	*	Transport of gliders
15.4.44	Transport	Barkston Heath	Shipsham	*	
15.4.44	Return	Shipsham	Barkston Heath	*	
20.4.44	Training	Barkston Heath	Barkston Heath	Moh	Towing of gliders
20.4.44	Training	Barkston Heath	Barkston Heath	Moh	Towing of gliders
21.4.44	Training	Barkston Heath	Barkston Heath	Moh/Martzen	Paratroop jump
22.4.44	Training	Barkston Heath	Barkston Heath	Moh	
22.4.44	Training	Barkston Heath	Barkston Heath	Moh	
23.4.44	Transport	Barkston Heath	Bottesford	Moh/Martzen	
23.4.44	*	Bottesford		Moh/Martzen	
23.4.44	Return		Barkston Heath	Moh/Martzen	
24.4.44	Transport	Barkston Heath	*	Moh/Martzen	
24.4.44	Transport	*	Cottesmore	Moh/Martzen	
24.4.44	Return	Cottes-more	Barkston Heath	Moh/Martzen	
27.4.44	Transport	Barkston Heath	Cottesmore	Moh/Martzen	

Continued overleaf

Continued

Date	Mission	Takeoff	Landing	Pilot	Notes
27.4.44	Return	Cottesmore	Barkston Heath	Moh/Martzen	
29.4.44	Training	Barkston Heath	Barkston Heath	Martzen	Formation flying
5.5.44	Training	Barkston Heath	Barkston Heath	Moh	Formation flying
11.5.44	Training	Barkston Heath	Barkston Heath	Moh	Paratroop jump, 5 hrs.' flight in darkness
12.5.44	Training	Barkston Heath	Barkston Heath	Moh	
12.5.44	Training	Barkston Heath	Barkston Heath	Moh	
16.5.44	Training	Barkston Heath	Barkston Heath	Moh	Flight time 30 mins.
17.5.44	Transport	Barkston Heath	Base 559	Moh	
17.5.44	Return	Base 559	Barkston Heath	Moh	
22.5.44	Training	Barkston Heath	Barkston Heath	Moh/Martzen	
22.5.44	Training	Barkston Heath	Barkston Heath	Moh/Martzen	
22.5.44	Training	Barkston Heath	Barkston Heath	Moh/Martzen	
23.5.44	Training	Barkston Heath	Fairford	Moh	Evacuation Training
23.5.44	Training	Fairford	*	Moh	Evacuation Training
23.5.44	Training	*	*	Moh	Evacuation Training
23.5.44	Training	*	Barkston Heath	Moh	Evacuation Training
26.5.44	Transport	Barkston Heath	Base 489	Moh	
26.5.44	Return	Base 489	Barkston Heath	*	
27.5.44	Training	Barkston Heath	Barkston Heath	Moh	Transport Training
27.5.44	Training	Barkston Heath	Barkston Heath	Moh	Transport Training
27.5.44	Training	Barkston Heath	Barkston Heath	Moh	Transport Training

Continued overleaf

Continued

Date	Mission	Takeoff	Landing	Pilot	Notes
27.5.44	Training	Barkston Heath	Barkston Heath	Moh	Transport Training
27.5.44	Training	Barkston Heath	Barkston Heath	Moh	Transport Training
27.5.44	Training	Barkston Heath	Barkston Heath	Moh	Transport Training
30.5.44	Training	Barkston Heath	Barkston Heath	Moh	Paratroop jump
30.5.44	Training	Barkston Heath	Barkston Heath	Moh	Paratroop jump
30.5.44	Training	Barkston Heath	Barkston Heath	Moh	Paratroop jump
30.5.44	Training	Barkston Heath	Barkston Heath	Moh	Paratroop jump
30.5.44	Training	Barkston Heath	Barkston Heath	Moh	Paratroop jump
30.5.44	Training	Barkston Heath	Barkston Heath	Moh	Paratroop jump
30.5.44	Training	Barkston Heath	Barkston Heath	Moh	Paratroop jump
30.5.44	Training	Barkston Heath	Barkston Heath	Moh	Paratroop jump
5/6.6.44	Combat flight	Barkston Heath	Barkston Heath	Moh	Paratroopers over Normandy. 5 hrs. 45 mins night flight.
19.6.44	Transport	Barkston Heath	Base 186	*	
19.6.44	Return	Base 186	Barkston Heath	*	
20.6.44	Combat transport	Barkston Heath	*	Moh	
20.6.44	Combat transport	*	Normandy	Moh	
20.6.44	Return	Normandy	Barkston Heath	Moh	
22.6.44	Transport	Barkston Heath	Base 466	Moh/Martzen	
22.6.44	Return	Base 466	Barkston Heath	*	
27.6.44	Training	Barkston Heath	Barkston Heath	Moh/Martzen	Transport Training
28.6.44	Training	Barkston Heath	Barkston Heath	Moh	Landing Training

Continued overleaf

Continued

Date	Mission	Takeoff	Landing	Pilot	Notes
28.6.44	Training	Barkston Heath	Barkston Heath	Moh	Landing Training
28.6.44	Training	Barkston Heath	Barkston Heath	Moh	Landing Training
28.6.44	Training	Barkston Heath	Barkston Heath	Moh	Landing Training
28.6.44	Training	Barkston Heath	Barkston Heath	Moh	Landing Training
29.6.44	Training	Barkston Heath	Barkston Heath	Moh	Landing Training
29.6.44	Training	Barkston Heath	Barkston Heath	Moh	Landing Training
29.6.44	Training	Barkston Heath	Barkston Heath	Moh	Landing Training
29.6.44	Training	Barkston Heath	Barkston Heath	Moh	Landing Training
29.6.44	Training	Barkston Heath	Barkston Heath	Moh	Landing Training
29.6.44	Training	Barkston Heath	Barkston Heath	Moh	Landing Training
4.7.44	Combat transport	Barkston Heath	*	Moh	
4.7.44	Combat transport	*	Normandy	Moh	
4.7.44	Return	Normandy	Barkston Heath	Moh	
6.7.44	Training	Barkston Heath	Barkston Heath	Moh	Towing of gliders
7.7.44	Training	Barkston Heath	Barkston Heath	Moh	Landing Training instruments
7.7.44	Training	Barkston Heath	Barkston Heath	Moh	Landing Training instruments
7.7.44	Training	Barkston Heath	Barkston Heath	Moh	Landing Training instruments
8.7.44	Medical transport	Barkston Heath	*	*	
8.7.44	Medical transport	*	Prestwick	*	
8.7.44	Return	Prestwick	Barkston Heath	*	
10.7.44	Training	Barkston Heath	Barkston Heath	Moh	Towing of gliders
10.7.44	Training	Barkston Heath	Barkston Heath	Moh	Towing of gliders
10.7.44	Training	Barkston Heath	Barkston Heath	Moh	Towing of gliders

Continued overleaf

Continued

Date	Mission	Takeoff	Landing	Pilot	Notes
11.7.44	Combat transport	Barkston Heath	Normandy	Moh	
11.7.44	Return	Normandy	Barkston Heath	Moh	
12.7.44	Training	Barkston Heath	Barkston Heath	Moh	Paratroop jump
14.7.44	Training	Barkston Heath	Barkston Heath	Moh	Formation flying
17.7.44	Training	Barkston Heath	Wittering	*	Formation flying
17.7.44	Training	Wittering	Barkston Heath	*	Formation flying
18.7.44	Combat transport	Barkston Heath	*	Moh/Martzen	
18.7.44	Combat transport	*	Normandy	Moh/Martzen	
18.7.44	Return	Normandy	Barkston Heath	Moh/Martzen	
19.7.44	Training	Barkston Heath	Wittering	Moh	Formation flying gliders
19.7.44	Training	Wittering	Wittering	Moh	Formation flying gliders
19.7.44	Training	Wittering	Barkston Heath	Moh	Formation flying gliders
20.7.44	Medical transport	Barkston Heath	*	Moh	
20.7.44	Medical transport	*	Prestwick	Moh	
20.7.44	Return	Prestwick	Barkston Heath	Moh	
24.7.44	Combat transport	Barkston Heath	*	Moh	
24.7.44	Combat transport	*	*	Moh	
24.7.44	Combat transport	*	*	Moh	
24.7.44	Combat transport	*	*	Moh	
24.7.44	Combat transport	*	*	Moh	
24.7.44	Combat transport	Normandy	Barkston Heath	Moh	
26.7.44	Training	Barkston Heath	Barkston Heath	Moh	Formation flying
26.7.44	Training	Barkston Heath	Barkston Heath	Moh	Formation flying
26.7.44	Training	Barkston Heath	Barkston Heath	Moh	Formation flying

Continued overleaf

Continued

Date	Mission	Takeoff	Landing	Pilot	Notes
28.7.44	Combat transport	Barkston Heath	*	Moh	
28.7.44	Combat transport	*	Normandy	Moh	
28.7.44	Return	Normandy	Barkston Heath	Moh	
29.7.44	Transport	Barkston Heath	Exeter	*	
29.7.44	Return	Exeter	Barkston Heath	*	
3.8.44	Training	Barkston Heath	Barkston Heath	*	Formation flying
5.8.44	Training	Barkston Heath	Barkston Heath	*	Formation flying
7.8.44	Training	Barkston Heath	Barkston Heath	Moh	Paratroop jump at night
8.8.44	Training	Barkston Heath	Barkston Heath	Moh	Paratroop jump
8.8.44	Training	Barkston Heath	Barkston Heath	Moh	Paratroop jump
8.8.44	Training	Barkston Heath	Barkston Heath	Moh	Paratroop jump
8.8.44	Training	Barkston Heath	Barkston Heath	Moh	Paratroop jump
10.8.44	Training	Barkston Heath	Barkston Heath	Moh/Martzen	
10.8.44	Training	Barkston Heath	Barkston Heath	Moh/Martzen	
10.8.44	Training	Barkston Heath	Barkston Heath	Moh/Martzen	
10.8.44	Training	Barkston Heath	Barkston Heath	Moh/Martzen	
11.8.44	Training	Barkston Heath	Barkston Heath	Moh	Troop landing
11.8.44	Training	Barkston Heath	Barkston Heath	Moh	Troop landing
12.8.44	Training	Barkston Heath	Barkston Heath	Moh	
12.8.44	Training	Barkston Heath	Barkston Heath	Moh	
12.8.44	Training	Barkston Heath	Barkston Heath	Moh	
12.8.44	Training	Barkston Heath	Barkston Heath	Moh	

Continued overleaf

Continued

Date	Mission	Takeoff	Landing	Pilot	Notes
12.8.44	Training	Barkston Heath	Barkston Heath	Moh	
12.8.44	Training	Barkston Heath	Barkston Heath	Moh	
12.8.44	Training	Barkston Heath	Barkston Heath	Moh	
13.8.44	Combat transport	Barkston Heath	*	Moh	
13.8.44	Combat transport	*	Normandy	Moh	
13.8.44	Return	Normandy	Barkston Heath	Moh	
14.8.44	Combat transport	Barkston Heath	Normandy	Moh	
14.8.44	Return	Normandy	Barkston Heath	Moh	
15.8.44	Combat transport	Barkston Heath	*	Moh	
15.8.44	Combat transport	*	Normandy	Moh	
15.8.44	Combat transport	Normandy	*	Moh	
15.8.44	Combat transport	*	*	Moh	
15.8.44	Combat transport	*	*	Moh	
15.8.44	Combat transport	*	Barkston Heath	Moh	
16.8.44	Combat transport	Barkston Heath	Normandy	*	
16.8.44	Combat transport	Normandy	Barkston Heath	*	
23.8.44	Medical transport	Barkston Heath	Prestwick	*	
23.8.44	Return	Prestwick	Barkston Heath	*	
24.8.44	Medical transport	Barkston Heath	*	Moh	
24.8.44	Medical transport	*	Prestwick	Moh	
24.8.44	Return	Prestwick	Barkston Heath	Moh	
24.8.44	Medical transport	Barkston Heath	*	Moh	
24.8.44	Medical transport	*	Prestwick	Moh	
24.8.44	Return	Prestwick	Barkston Heath	Moh	

Continued overleaf

Continued

Date	Mission	Takeoff	Landing	Pilot	Notes
25.8.44	Combat transport	Barkston Heath	Base 466	Moh	
25.8.44	Combat transport	*	*	Moh	
25.8.44	Combat transport	Normandy	*	Moh	
25.8.44	Combat transport	*	Barkston Heath		
28.8.44	Training	Barkston Heath	Barkston Heath	Moh	Paratroop jump
11.9.44	Combat transport	Barkston Heath	*	Moh	
11.9.44	Combat transport	*	*	Moh	
11.9.44	Combat transport	Belgium	*	Moh	
11.9.44	Combat transport	*	Barkston Heath	Moh	
12.9.44	Transport	Barkston Heath	Kemble	Moh	
12.9.44	Return	Kemble	Barkston Heath	*	
13.9.44	Combat transport	Barkston Heath	Base 58 (Belgium)	Moh	
13.9.44	Combat transport	Base 58 (Belgium)	*	Moh	
13.9.44	Combat transport	*	Barkston Heath	Moh	
17.9.44	Combat flight	Barkston Heath	Barkston Heath	Moh	Paratroopers over Drop Zone "Z", W. Oosterbeek
23.9.44	Combat flight	Barkston Heath	Barkston Heath	Moh	Troop landing by glider Landing Zone "O", N. Grave
29.9.44	Combat transport	Barkston Heath	Belgium	*	
29.9.44	Return	Belgium	Barkston Heath	*	
12 el. 13.5.45	Transit	Barkston Heath (?)	Trinidad		Landing 16.5.44
23.9.45	Transit	Trinidad	Morrison, Florida	*	
24.10.45	Transit	Morrison, Florida	Bush Field, Georgia	*	Mothballed

* No information

Appendix 3

Specifications for Douglas C-47A Skytrain

Powerplant: 2 air-cooled 14-cylinder Pratt & Whitney R-1830-90C Twin Wasp radial engines
Engine capacity: 1,200 hp at takeoff
Max speed: 224 mph/10,000 ft
Cruising speed: 160 mph
Service ceiling: 26,400 ft
Range: 1,600 miles

Wingspan: 95 ft 6 in
Wing area: 987 ft2
Length: 63 ft 9 in
Height: 17 ft

Crew: 4 men
Passengers: 21-36 men (18 fully equipped paratroopers)
Payload: 6,000 lb

Empty weight: 18,135 lb
Loaded weight: 26,000 lb

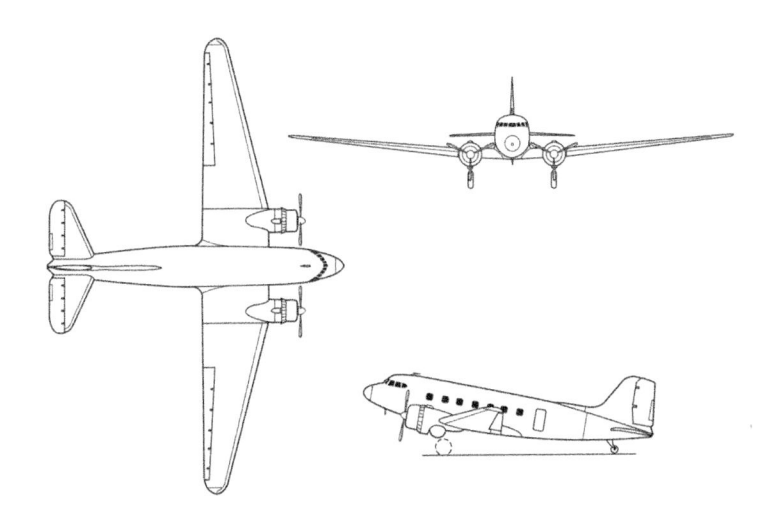

Sources

I. Archives

61st Troop Carrier Group History.
AAF Sta 483. Squadron History—Fourteenth Troop Carrier Squadron, AAF, Maxwell Air Force Base, USA.
AFHRA (Air Force Historical Research Agency), Maxwell Air Force Base, USA.
Airborne Assault Archive, Duxford, UK.
Bundesarchiv-Militärarchiv, Freiburg, Germany.
Gelders Archief, Arnhem, The Netherlands.
Liddell Hart Centre for Military Archives, King's College, London, UK.
NARA (National Archives and Records Administration), Washington, DC, USA.
NIOD (Nederlands Instituut voor Oorlogsdocumentatie), The Hague, The Netherlands.

II. Literature

Balke, Ulf. *Der Luftkrieg in Europa 1941-1945*. Bechtermünz Verlag, Augsburg 1997.
Bergström, Christer. *Arnhem 1944 – An Epic Battle Revisited. Vol. 1: Tanks and Paratroopers*. Vaktel förlag, Eskilstuna, Sweden, 2019.
Bergström, Christer. *Arnhem 1944 – An Epic Battle Revisited. Vol. 2: The Lost Victory. September-October 1944*. Vaktel förlag, Eskilstuna, Sweden, 2019.
Hicks, Norman. *Captured at Arnhem*. Pen & Sword, Barnsley 2013.
Liddle, Peter (ed). *D-Day: By Those Who Were There*. Pen & Sword, Barnsley 2004.
LoFaro Guy. *The Sword of St Michael: The 82nd Airborne Division in World War II*. Da Capo Press, Cambridge, MA 2011.
Moore, Charles. *Margaret Thatcher: The Authorized Biography. Volume One: Not for Turning*. Allen Lane/Penguin Groups, London 2013.
Mrozek, Steven J. *82nd Airborne Division*. Turner Publishing, 1987.
Harrison, Mark. (ed.) *The Economics of World War II*. Cambridge University Press, Cambridge 1998.
Roach, Clyde E. *Confessions of an Airline Pilot*. Venture Print, Plymouth, NH 1998.
Schipske, Gerrie. *Rosie the Riveter in Long Beach*. Arcadia Publishing, Charleston 2008.
Warren, Dr. John. *Airborne Operations in World War II, European Theater. USAF Historical Studies No. 97*. USAF Historical Division, Research Studies Institute, Air University 1956.

III. Periodicals

The Des Moines Tribune.
Grantham News Chronicle.
Grantham Journal.

IV. Internet Sources

61st Troop Carrier Group by Kevin King. ww2flyers53rdtc.com
RAF Barkston Heath Research Group. raf-barkston-heath.

Notes

[1] AFHRA, Maxwell Air Force Base. 61st Troop Carrier Group War Diary.
[2] "Missions" by Willis W. Mitchell. *61st Troop Carrier Group History*, p. 274. Via Kevin King
[3] Via Kevin King.
[4] Mrozek, *82nd Airborne Division,* p. 35.
[5] Field Order Number 1. 6 June 1944. Neptune. HQ Sixty First Troop Carrier Group. Via Cheryl (Moh) Grau & Brett Grau.
[6] Via Cheryl (Moh) Grau & Brett Grau.
[7] Via Cheryl (Moh) Grau & Brett Grau.
[8] Roach, *Confessions of an Airline Pilot,* p. 24.
[9] *61st Troop Carrier Group History,* p. 274. Via Kevin King.
[10] Mrozek, *82nd Airborne Division,* p. 35.
[11] Liddle, *D-Day: By Those Who Were There,* p. 59.
[12] Warren, *Airborne Operations in World War II, European Theater,* p. 55.
[13] Liddle, *D-Day: By Those Who Were There,* p. 59.
[14] *61st Troop Carrier Group History,* p. 274. Via Kevin King.
[15] *61st Troop Carrier Group History,* p. 276. Via Kevin King.
[16] AAF Sta 483. Squadron History—Fourteenth Troop Carrier Squadron, AAF. 1 May 1943 to 31 May 1943. Via Tom Martin.
[17] Via Kevin King.
[18] "Missions" by Virgil L. Cox. *61st Troop Carrier Group History*, p. 11. Via Kevin King.
[19] NARA. Individual Flight Record. Ser. No. 732050. Moh, Norbert D. Month: May 1943.
[20] AAF Sta 483. Squadron History—Fourteenth Troop Carrier Squadron, AAF. 1 May 1943 to 31 May 1943. Via Tom Martin.
[21] "Missions" by William I. Marlatt. *61st Troop Carrier Group History*, p. 15. Via Kevin King.
[22] AFHRA, Maxwell Air Force Base. 61st Troop Carrier Group War Diary.
[23] *61st Troop Carrier Group History,* p. 16. Via Kevin King.
[24] AAF Sta 483. Squadron History—Fourteenth Troop Carrier Squadron, AAF. 1 May 1943 to 31 May 1943. Via Tom Martin.
[25] Via Cheryl (Moh) Grau.
[26] AAF Sta 483. Squadron History—Fourteenth Troop Carrier Squadron, AAF. 1 June 1943 to 30 June 1943. Via Tom Martin.
[27] "Missions" by William I. Marlatt. *61st Troop Carrier Group History*, p. 24. Via Kevin King.
[28] AAF Sta 483. Squadron History—Fourteenth Troop Carrier Squadron, AAF. 1 July 1943 to 31 July 1943. Via Tom Martin.
[29] Via Cheryl (Moh) Grau.
[30] Via Cheryl (Moh) Grau.
[31] AAF Sta 483. Squadron History—Fourteenth Troop Carrier Squadron, AAF. 1 July 1943 to 31 July 1943. Via Tom Martin.
[32] Via Cheryl (Moh) Grau.
[33] NARA. Individual Flight Record. Ser. No. 732050. Moh, Norbert D. Month: August 1943.
[34] AAF Sta 483. Squadron History—Fourteenth Troop Carrier Squadron, AAF. 1 September 1943 to 30 September 1943. Via Tom Martin.
[35] NARA. Individual Flight Record. Ser. No. 732050. Moh, Norbert D. Month: September 1943.
[36] AAF Sta 483. Squadron History—Fourteenth Troop Carrier Squadron, AAF. 1 September 1943 to 30 September 1943. Via Tom Martin.

[37] LoFaro, *The Sword of St. Michael*, p. 142.
[38] NARA. Individual Flight Record. Ser. No. 732050. Moh, Norbert D.
[39] AAF Sta 483. Squadron History — Fourteenth Troop Carrier Squadron, AAF. 1 October 1943 to 31 October1943. Via Tom Martin.
[40] James F. Shemas in *61st Troop Carrier Group History*, p. 107. Via Kevin King.
[41] Harrison, *The Economics of World War II*, p. 10.
[42] Schipske, *Rosie the Riveter in Long Beach*, p. 60.
[43] US Air Force Record Card. Model C-47. Serial Number 43-30732. Date Received: 10-5-43. Via Tom Martin.
[44] US Air Force Record Card. Model C-47. Serial Number 43-30732. Date Received: 10-5-43. Via Tom Martin.
[45] US Air Force Record Card. Model C-47. Serial Number 43-30732. Date Received: 10-5-43. Via Tom Martin.
[46] AAF Sta 483. Squadron History — Fourteenth Troop Carrier Squadron, AAF. 1 December 1943 to 31 December 1943. Via Tom Martin.
[47] AAF Sta 483. Squadron History — Fourteenth Troop Carrier Squadron, AAF. 1 December 1943 to 31 December 1943. Via Tom Martin.
[48] AAF Sta 483. Squadron History — Fourteenth Troop Carrier Squadron, AAF. 1 December 1943 to 31 December 1943. Via Tom Martin.
[49] NARA. Individual Flight Record. Ser. No. 732050. Moh, Norbert D. Month: May 1943.
[50] AAF Sta 483. Squadron History — Fourteenth Troop Carrier Squadron, AAF. 1 February 1944 to 29 February 1944. Via Tom Martin
[51] Via Cheryl (Moh) Grau.
[52] Via Cheryl (Moh) Grau.
[53] NARA. Individual Flight Record. Ser. No. 732050. Moh, Norbert D.
[54] 1st Lt Lester G. Carson in *61st Troop Carrier Group History*, p. 179. Via Kevin King.
[55] AAF Sta 483. Squadron History — Fourteenth Troop Carrier Squadron, AAF. 1 February 1944 to 29 February 1944. Via Tom Martin.
[56] Via Kevin King.
[57] Via Kevin King.
[58] AAF Sta 483. Squadron History — Fourteenth Troop Carrier Squadron, AAF. 1 February 1944 to 29 February 1944. Via Tom Martin.
[59] Wikipedia: Barkston Heath Royal Air Force Base. https://sv.wikipedia.org/wiki/Barkston_Heath_Royal_Air_Force_Base
[60] *61st Troop Carrier Group History*, p. 182. Via Kevin King.
[61] AAF Sta 483. Squadron History — Fourteenth Troop Carrier Squadron, AAF. 1 February 1944 to 29 February 1944. Via Tom Martin.
[62] Personal Diary of Charles N. Fay, via Catherine Roberts, p. 30. RAF Barkston Heath Research Group. http://raf-barkston-heath.forumotion.co.uk/t437-personal-diary-of-charles-n-fay.
[63] *61st Troop Carrier Group History*, p. 177. Via Kevin King.
[64] AAF Sta 483. Squadron History — Fourteenth Troop Carrier Squadron, AAF. 1 March 1944 to 31 March 1944. Via Tom Martin.
[65] NARA. Individual Flight Record. Ser. No. 732050. Moh, Norbert D. Month: March 1944.
[66] NARA. Individual Flight Record. Ser. No. 732050. Moh, Norbert D. Month: March 1944.
[67] NARA. Individual Flight Record. Ser. No. 732050. Moh, Norbert D. Month: March 1944.
[68] AAF Sta 483. Squadron History — Fourteenth Troop Carrier Squadron, AAF. 1 March 1944 to 31 March 1944. Via Tom Martin.
[69] NARA. Individual Flight Record. Ser. No. 732050. Moh, Norbert D. Month: March 1944; AAF Sta 483. Squadron History—Fourteenth Troop Carrier Squadron, AAF. 1 March 1944 to 31 March 1944. Via Tom Martin.

[70] NARA. Individual Flight Record. Ser. No. 732050. Moh, Norbert D. Month: March 1944.
[71] AAF Sta 483. Squadron History — Fourteenth Troop Carrier Squadron, AAF. 1 March 1944 to 31 March 1944. Via Tom Martin.
[72] AAF Sta 483. Squadron History — Fourteenth Troop Carrier Squadron, AAF. 1 March 1944 to 31 March 1944. Via Tom Martin.
[73] Balke, *Der Luftkrieg in Europa 1941-1945*, p. 321.
[74] AFHRA, Maxwell Air Force Base. 61st Troop Carrier Group War Diary.
[75] NARA. Individual Flight Record. Ser. No. 732050. Moh, Norbert D. Month: March 1944.
[76] AAF Sta 483. Squadron History — Fourteenth Troop Carrier Squadron, AAF. 1 March 1944 to 31 March 1944. Via Tom Martin.
[77] NARA. Individual Flight Record. Ser. No. 732050. Moh, Norbert D. Month: March 1944.
[78] NARA. Individual Flight Record. Ser. No. 732050. Moh, Norbert D. Month: March 1944.
[79] *61st Troop Carrier Group History*, p. 216. Via Kevin King.
[80] NARA. Individual Flight Record. Ser. No. 732050. Moh, Norbert D. Month: March 1944.
[81] NARA. Individual Flight Record. Ser. No. 732050. Moh, Norbert D. Month: March 1944.
[82] AFHRA, Maxwell Air Force Base. 61st Troop Carrier Group War Diary.
[83] NARA. Individual Flight Record. Ser. No. 732050. Moh, Norbert D. Month: March 1944.
[84] NARA. Individual Flight Record. Ser. No. 732050. Moh, Norbert D. Month: April 1944.
[85] AFHRA, Maxwell Air Force Base. 61st Troop Carrier Group War Diary.
[86] AFHRA, Maxwell Air Force Base. 61st Troop Carrier Group War Diary.
[87] AAF Sta 483. Squadron History—Fourteenth Troop Carrier Squadron, AAF. 1 April 1944 to 30 April 1944. Via Tom Martin; NARA. Individual Flight Record. Ser. No. 732050. Moh, Norbert D. Month: April 1944.
[88] NARA. Individual Flight Record. Ser. No. 732050. Moh, Norbert D. Month: April 1944.
[89] NARA. Individual Flight Record. Ser. No. 732050. Moh, Norbert D. Month: April 1944.
[90] AAF Sta 483. Squadron History—Fourteenth Troop Carrier Squadron, AAF. 1 April 1944 to 30 April 1944. Via Tom Martin.
[91] NARA. Individual Flight Record. Ser. No. 732050. Moh, Norbert D. Month: April 1944.
[92] AAF Sta 483. Squadron History—Fourteenth Troop Carrier Squadron, AAF. 1 April 1944 to 30 April 1944. Via Tom Martin.
[93] Grantham News Chronicle, June 5, 1944.
[94] Moore, *Margaret Thatcher: The Authorized Biography. Volume One: Not for Turning*, p. 15.
[95] Moore, *Margaret Thatcher: The Authorized Biography. Volume One: Not for Turning*, p. 16.
[96] Personal Diary of Charles N. Fay, via Catherine Roberts, p. 31. RAF Barkston Heath Research Group. http://raf-barkston-heath.forumotion.co.uk/t437-personal-diary-of-charles-n-fay.
[97] NARA. Individual Flight Record. Ser. No. 732050. Moh, Norbert D. Month: May 1944.
[98] AAF Sta 483. Squadron History—Fourteenth Troop Carrier Squadron, AAF. 1 May 1944 to 31 May 1944. Via Tom Martin.
[99] *61st Troop Carrier Group History*, p. 245. Via Kevin King.
[100] LoFaro, *The Sword of St. Michael*, p. 187.
[101] AAF Sta 483. Squadron History—Fourteenth Troop Carrier Squadron, AAF. 1 May 1944 to 31 May 1944. Via Tom Martin.
[102] NARA. Individual Flight Record. Ser. No. 732050. Moh, Norbert D. Month: May 1944.
[103] NARA. Individual Flight Record. Ser. No. 732050. Moh, Norbert D. Month: May 1944.
[104] NARA. Individual Flight Record. Ser. No. 732050. Moh, Norbert D. Month: May 1944.
[105] AAF Sta 483. Squadron History—Fourteenth Troop Carrier Squadron, AAF. 1 May 1944 to 31 May 1944. Via Tom Martin.
[106] NARA. Individual Flight Record. Ser. No. 732050. Moh, Norbert D. Month: May 1944.
[107] AFHRA, Maxwell Air Force Base. 61st Troop Carrier Group War Diary.

[108] AAF Sta 483. Squadron History—Fourteenth Troop Carrier Squadron, AAF. 1 May 1944 to 31 May 1944. Via Tom Martin.
[109] James F. Shemas in *61st Troop Carrier Group History*, pp. 271f. Via Kevin King.
[110] Field Order Number 1. 6 June 1944. Neptune-Bigot. HQ Sixty First Troop Carrier Group. Via Cheryl (Moh) Grau & Brett Grau.
[111] James F. Shemas in *61st Troop Carrier Group History*, p. 272. Via Kevin King.
[112] AAF Sta 483. Squadron History—Fourteenth Troop Carrier Squadron, AAF. 1 June 1944 to 30 June1944. Via Tom Martin.
[113] NARA. Individual Flight Record. Ser. No. 732050. Moh, Norbert D. Month: June 1944.
[114] AAF Sta 483. Squadron History—Fourteenth Troop Carrier Squadron, AAF. 1 June 1944 to 30 June 1944. Via Tom Martin.
[115] NARA. Individual Flight Record. Ser. No. 732050. Moh, Norbert D. Month: June 1944.
[116] NARA. Individual Flight Record. Ser. No. 732050. Moh, Norbert D. Month: July 1944.
[117] NARA. Individual Flight Record. Ser. No. 732050. Moh, Norbert D. Month: July 1944.
[118] AAF Sta 483. Squadron History—Fourteenth Troop Carrier Squadron, AAF. 1 July 1944 to 3031 July 1944. Via Tom Martin.
[119] AAF Sta 483. Squadron History—Fourteenth Troop Carrier Squadron, AAF. 1 July 1944 to 31 July 1944. Via Tom Martin.
[120] NARA. Individual Flight Record. Ser. No. 732050. Moh, Norbert D. Month: July 1944.
[121] AFHRA, Maxwell Air Force Base. 61st Troop Carrier Group War Diary.
[122] *61st Troop Carrier Group History*, p. 320. Via Kevin King.
[123] NARA. Individual Flight Record. Ser. No. 732050. Moh, Norbert D. Month: July 1944.
[124] NARA. Individual Flight Record. Ser. No. 732050. Moh, Norbert D. Month: August 1944.
[125] AAF Sta 483. Squadron History — Fourteenth Troop Carrier Squadron, AAF. 1 August 1944 to 31 August 1944. Via Tom Martin.
[126] NARA. Individual Flight Record. Ser. No. 732050. Moh, Norbert D. Month: August 1944.
[127] AAF Sta 483. Squadron History — Fourteenth Troop Carrier Squadron, AAF. 1 August 1944 to 31 August 1944. Via Tom Martin.
[128] NARA. Individual Flight Record. Ser. No. 732050. Moh, Norbert D. Month: August 1944.
[129] AAF Sta 483. Squadron History — Fourteenth Troop Carrier Squadron, AAF. 1 August 1944 to 31 August 1944. Via Tom Martin; NARA. Individual Flight Record. Ser. No. 732050. Moh, Norbert D. Month: August 1944.
[130] AAF Sta 483. Squadron History — Fourteenth Troop Carrier Squadron, AAF. 1 August 1944 to 31 August 1944. Via Tom Martin; NARA. Individual Flight Record. Ser. No. 732050. Moh, Norbert D. Month: August 1944.
[131] AAF Sta 483. Squadron History—Fourteenth Troop Carrier Squadron, AAF. 1 September 1944 to 30 September 1944. Via Tom Martin; NARA. Individual Flight Record. Ser. No. 732050. Moh, Norbert D. Month: September 1944.
[132] Via Cheryl (Moh) Grau.
[133] AAF Sta 483. Squadron History—Fourteenth Troop Carrier Squadron, AAF. 1 September 1944 to 30 September 1944.
[134] Hicks, *Captured at Arnhem*, p. 156.
[135] Airborne Assault Archive. Box 4F1, 2/10/4. File No. 48, Arnhem. Major Gen G.W. Lathbury. Arnhem Diary September-October 1944.
[136] Hicks, *Captured at Arnhem*, pp. 156f.
[137] Airborne Assault Archive. Box 4F2 2/10/10. Arnhem 1944 Veterans Club. Letter from Mrs. Belinda Brinton 18-2-98.
[138] Airborne Assault Archive. Box 4F1, 2/10/4. File No. 48, Arnhem. Major Gen G.W. Lathbury. Arnhem Diary September-October 1944.

[139] AAF Sta 483. Squadron History—Fourteenth Troop Carrier Squadron, AAF. 1 September 1944 to 30 September 1944.
[140] Airborne Assault Archive. Box 4F1, 2/10/4. File No. 48, Arnhem. Major Gen G.W. Lathbury. Arnhem Diary September-October 1944.
[141] Airborne Assault Archive. Box 4F1, 2/10/4. File 54/61, Arnhem. 14217084 Sgt Cox BE 3 Plt. A' Coy 3 Para. Into Arnhem—Day One by Bruce Cox.
[142] AFHRA, Maxwell Air Force Base. 61st Troop Carrier Group War Diary.
[143] Nederlands Instituut voor Oorlogsdocumentatie (NIOD), Amsterdam. Identificatiecode 001. Wehrmachtbefehlshaber in den Niederlanden.
[144] Gelders Archief. Dokument 2171. Collectie Boeree. 1. 11. "The History of 7 Battalion K.O.S.B. in the Battle of Arnhem by Th.A. Boeree", 1954. Eén band, 103 genummerde bladen, afbeeldingen, kaarten, p. 26.
[145] King's College London. Liddell Hart Centre for Military Archives. 15/15: Papers of Reginald William Winchester ('Chester') Wilmot (1911-1954). 15/15/50/1. Notes from official sources and interrogation of Gen Kurt Student, Cdr 1 German Parachute Army on the German tactical response.
[146] Bergström, *Arnhem 1944: Slaget om Holland, Del 1*, p. 160.
[147] AFHRA, Maxwell Air Force Base. 61st Troop Carrier Group War Diary.
[148] AFHRA, Maxwell Air Force Base. 61st Troop Carrier Group War Diary.
[149] Airborne Assault Archive. Box 4F1, 2/10/4. File 54/61, Arnhem. 14217084 Sgt Cox BE 3 Plt. A' Coy 3 Para. Into Arnhem—Day One by Bruce Cox.
[150] Bergström, *Arnhem 1944: Slaget om Holland, Del 1*, p. 158.
[151] Via Cheryl (Moh) Grau.
[152] AFHRA, Maxwell Air Force Base. 61st Troop Carrier Group War Diary.
[153] AAF Sta 483. Squadron History—Fourteenth Troop Carrier Squadron, AAF. 1 September 1944 to 30 September 1944. Via Tom Martin.
[154] AAF Sta 483. Squadron History—Fourteenth Troop Carrier Squadron, AAF. 1 September 1944 to 30 September 1944. Via Tom Martin.
[155] AAF Sta 483. Squadron History—Fourteenth Troop Carrier Squadron, AAF. 1 September 1944 to 30 September 1944. Via Tom Martin; NARA. Individual Flight Record. Ser. No. 732050. Moh, Norbert D. Month: September 1944.
[156] Via Cheryl (Moh) Grau.
[157] Bundesarchiv-Militärarchiv N 756/270. Richter, Friedrich. "Brückenkopf bei Veghel."
[158] Via Cheryl (Moh) Grau.
[159] NARA. Individual Flight Record. Ser. No. 732050. Moh, Norbert D. Month: September 1944.
[160] AAF Sta 483. Squadron History—Fourteenth Troop Carrier Squadron, AAF. 1 September 1944 to 30 September 1944. Via Tom Martin.
[161] AAF Sta 483. Squadron History—Fourteenth Troop Carrier Squadron, AAF. Via Tom Martin.
[162] Via Cheryl (Moh) Grau.
[163] *61st Troop Carrier Group History*, p. 507. Via Kevin King.
[164] Via Cheryl (Moh) Grau.
[165] *The Des Moines Tribune* [Des Moines, Iowa] Thursday July 21, 1977. Via Kevin King.
[166] AFHRA, Maxwell Air Force Base. 61st Troop Carrier Group War Diary.
[167] US Air Force Record Card. Model C-47. Serial Number 43-30732. Date Received: 10-5-43. Via Tom Martin.

SOME OTHER AVAILABLE BOOKS BY THE AUTHOR

Christer Bergström enjoys the reputation of being one of the world's foremost experts on World War II. He has published 31 books on the subject, most of them in English. Through his indepth research work, he has moved the borders of our knowledge forward in many fields – e.g. the Ardennes offensive, the Battle of Britain, the Eastern Front, and Operation Market Garden.

BLACK CROSS RED STAR
– AIR WAR OVER THE EASTERN FRONT VOLUME 4
STALINGRAD TO KUBAN 1942–1943

Christer Bergström
400 pages
Large format, heavily illustrated

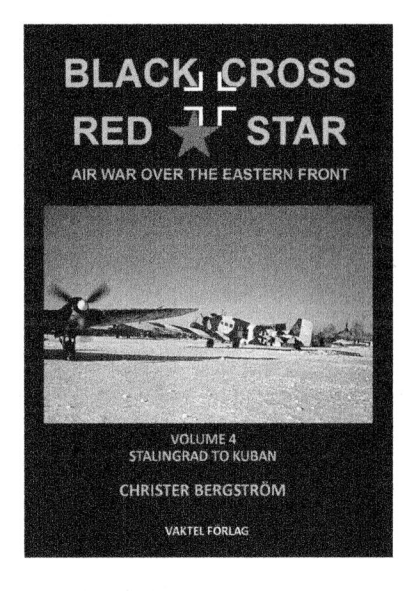

Regarded as the standard work on the air war over the Eastern Front during the Second World War, Christer Bergström's unique Black Cross/Red Star series covers the history of the air war on the Eastern Front in close detail, from the perspectives of both sides. Based on a close study of German and Russian archive material, as well as interviews with a large number of the airmen who participated in this aerial conflict, it has established itself as the main source on the air war on the Eastern Front.

Black Cross/Red Star, Volume 4 covers the air war along the entire Eastern Front during the winter period of 1942–1943 through March 1943, in great detail, with a balance between German and Soviet archive sources etc, and with many first-hand accounts.

U.K. is hard cover and contains colour profiles. ISBN 978-91-88441-21-8.
U.S. edition paperback and entirely b&w (except for the cover). ISBN 978-91-88441-50-8.

ARNHEM 1944
– AN EPIC BATTLE REVISITED.
VOL. 1: TANKS AND PARATROOPERS

Christer Bergström
400 pages

This is the ultimate book on "Operation Market Garden", by internationally highly acclaimed military historian Christer Bergström.

The indepth research made by the author has resulted in many myths and misconceptions being convincingly dispelled, backed up by detailed source notes. In fact, this two-volume book form a completely new image of the battle in the Netherlands in the autumn of 1944.

"Well-written, captivating and detailed … describes the brutal reality of war, which nevertheless does not have any negative impact on the dramatic description. A most exciting reading experience."
– Svensk Bibliotekstjänst (Swedish Library Service), on Volume 1.

U.K. edition, hard cover and size 210 x 155 mm ISBN 978-91-88441-44-7
U.S. edition, paperback and size 229 x 152 mm (6.00" x 9.00") ISBN 978-91-88441-48-5

ARNHEM 1944
– AN EPIC BATTLE REVISITED.
VOL. 2: THE LOST VICTORY. SEPTEMBER-OCTOBER 1944

Christer Bergström
440 pages

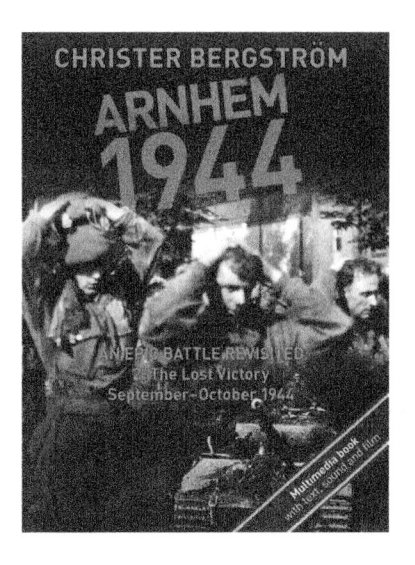

All previous published accounts of Operation "Market Garden" end the main story with the evacuation of the British airborne troops from Oosterbeek – which obscures the fact that Operation Market Garden at that time was still to be regarded as essentially a great success. It was only due to the following development of events (including the battle at Overloon in October 1944) that meant that the strategic success of Operation Market Garden could not be utilized to end the war before the turn of the year 1944.

"Military-historian Christer Bergström treats the source material with excellence and puts common images and myths of this battle into question. An extensive source and note list, photos, fact boxes, QR-coded film and sound clips supplement the text of this impressive work in two volumes about operation Market Garden. In summary - brilliant."
              – Svensk Bibliotekstjänst (Swedish Library Service), on Volume 2.

U.K. edition hard cover and size 210 x 155 mm ISBN 978-91-88441-45-4
U.S. edition paperback and size 229 x 152 mm (6.00" x 9.00") ISBN 978-91-88441-49-2

To be published in September 2019

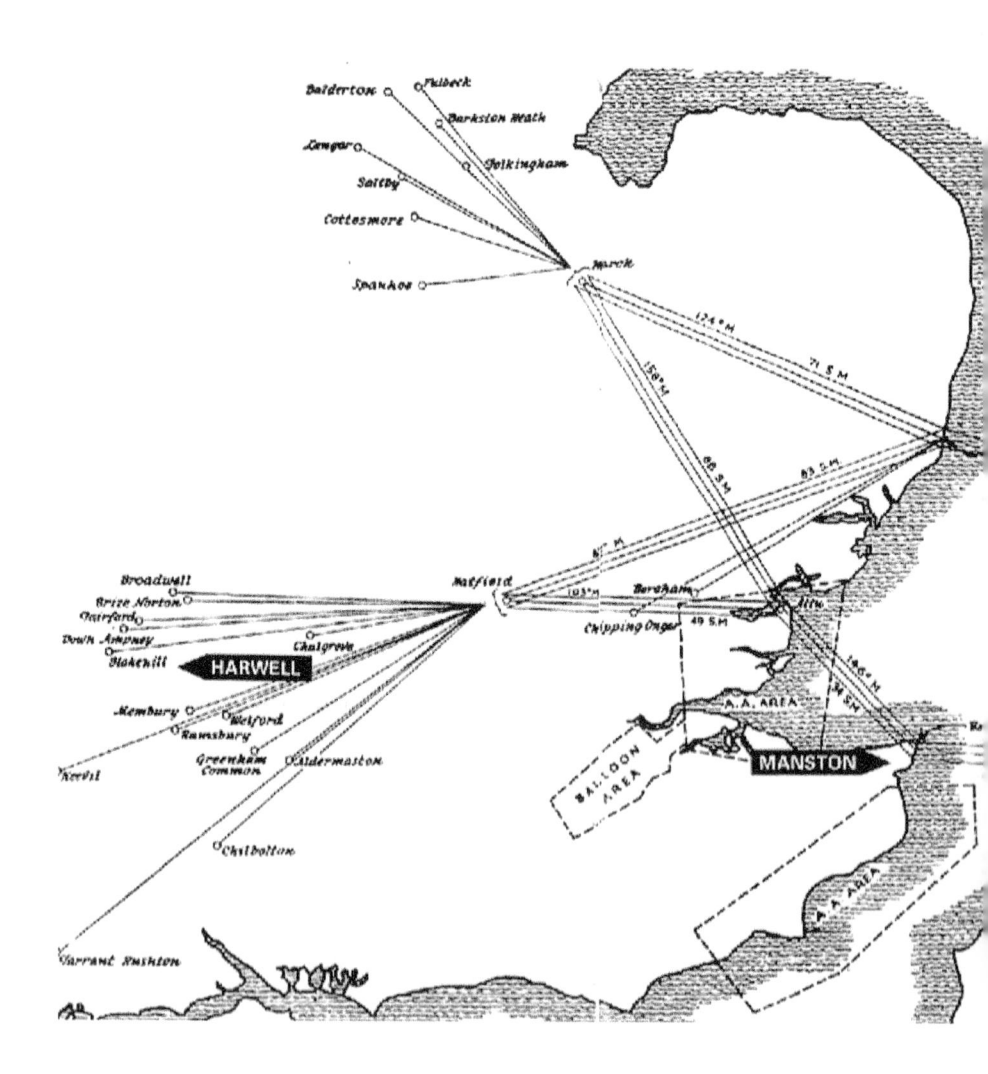

Flight route during Operation Market Garden, September 17, 1944

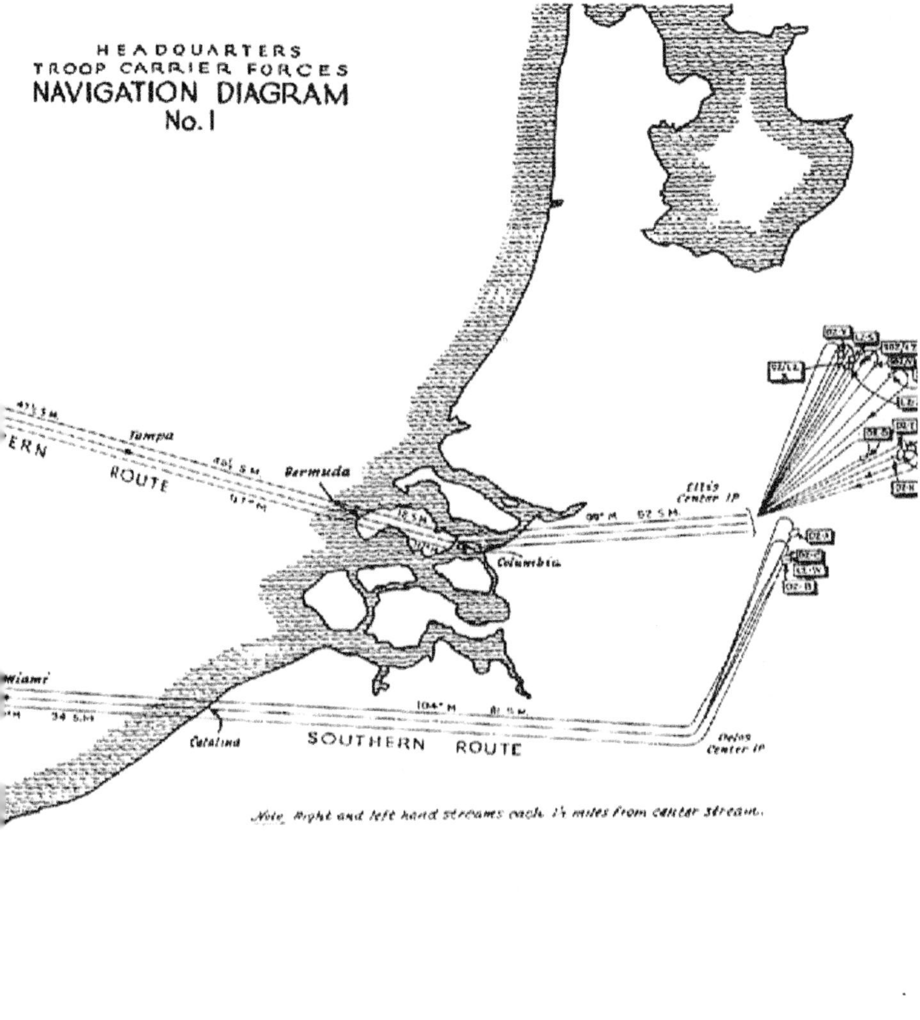
HEADQUARTERS
TROOP CARRIER FORCES
NAVIGATION DIAGRAM
No. 1
Tampa
ROUTE
Bermuda
Ellis
Center IP
Columbia
Miami
Catalina
SOUTHERN ROUTE
Delos
Center IP
Note, Right and left hand streams each 1½ miles from center stream.